Be sure to do the exercises of the

Dean Gemma Azan, *dean of the Christian International Ministry Training College*

We live in a world where the truth of the Word is hidden in the blindfolds of life. Life and circumstances have encumbered us, causing us to believe a lie. Paul's book is a bold approach, encouraging the believer to be accountable to remove the blindfolds. Be prepared to be challenged and to evaluate yourself. You will see the revelation of Truth—not only of the Word of God but of who you really are. If you grasp the truth in this book/workbook, you will have a renewed vision of life, of the body of Christ and of yourself. Paul's passion is evident for the Body of Christ to be free, to live to their full potential, and to know that they are not just loved but are born of the Beloved.

Apostle Leon Walters, *pastor of Christian International Central Family Worship Center, director of the Heartland Region of Christian International*

The Author has done an excellent job! He presents the truth of God's Word in such a manner that Christians can see themselves as more vital in the Kingdom of God here on earth. This truth will Awaken the Church!

I found the message in this book to be both challenging and inviting! I felt invited into more understanding of the truth of God's Word. I saw anew its effectiveness in our life today as the Body of Christ.

This book is designed to Awaken us from any slumber and to take our rightful place as God's representatives here on earth. This is a book that prepares Christians to be the first responders to God's glory, so we can meet the needs of a changing world in challenging times.

Apostles Dave & Linda Roeder, *deans of Christian International Central Ministry Equipping School*

This study book is ideal for both individuals and groups of people who are hungry for more of God. As you read Paul's prescriptive arguments, be prepared to see some old mindsets dislodged. He has written a persuasive, Scripturally-based manuscript, and he punctuates the book with a beautiful exhortation to embrace our place in the Father's heart.

Bishop Manuel Pate, *bishop of TN Valley Conference, International Pentecostal Holiness Church*

Have you ever felt like something was missing in your Christian life...like there was something more, but you couldn't figure it out? This book offers insights and practical applications to move you from being a hearer of the Word to a doer of the Word. It helps you remove the blindfolds that holds you back from your full potential in Christ. You will gain an understanding into your true identity, calling and gifting in the Body of Christ. The "truth that sets you free" is the heartbeat that burns in the pages of this book. May Christ be formed within you as you read it...for that truly is the hope of glory!

Bryan Cothran, *Founder and CEO of Cothran Capital LLC, Memphis, TN*

Praise God for His blessing on you and I am so excited what He will do in the lives of everyone who reads the book. As believers begin to see themselves the way God sees them and not just "rotten sinners saved by grace", a new era in the church will unfold!

Prophet & Pastor Bill & LaRue Lackie, *director of Prophetic Teams at Christian International*

What I have read in Paul's book has impacted me in my heart, soul and spirit. I am an avid reader and I found Paul's examples to be believable, well-related to his subject. Paul's references to scriptures relate readers right back to God's Word for each truth he conveys.

When I read something that is written by someone I personally know, and when I can hear their voice speaking the words, I am hooked to the end--and I am hooked on Paul's book, *Christian, What Are You? Removing the Blindfolds*.

Neither I nor Prophet Bill take it lightly to be included on the birthing of this book by Paul and Diane because I know they discussed it so thoroughly together. We love Paul & Diane. We love their vision. We know that this inviting book will touch many.

Our best to the Renfroes and their family!

Apostle Tom Hamon, *co-pastor of Vision Church@Christian International*

Paul Renfroe has written a practical guide and discourse pointed to challenge you about your spiritual identity, growth and maturity. This book will cause you to evaluate your self-perception in light of the Word of God, and your life style and attitudes in comparison to God's high calling on your life.

Apostle Jane Hamon, *co-pastor of Vision Church@Christian International*

In *Christian, What Are You? Removing the Blindfolds,* Paul Renfroe offers an insightful look into how God's Word describes the realities of what the Christian's life should exemplify. In our Western world our minds have been filled with secularized, materialistic, religious viewpoints that prevent us from embracing a spirit-directed, supernatural lifestyle as the "norm" for each and every Believer. In this book Paul not only confronts these world views in light of scripture, but also issues challenging activations that the reader can use to examine his or her own life and Christian walk and be empowered by God's truth.

Kayla -
This book challenges heavily fused church people and many have refused it without you, without it will that baggage be a great way it closer to get to GOD!

P

CHRISTIAN, WHAT ARE YOU?

REMOVING THE BLINDFOLDS

BY PAUL RENFROE

Purpose: for you to believe God's revelation in Scripture of your identity, characteristics, authority and place as a spirit made alive.

Christian, What Are You

Published by:
Christian International
177 Apostles Way
Santa Rosa Beach, FL 32459
www.christianinternational.com

In Partnership with:
A Book's Mind
PO Box 272847
Fort Collins, CO 80527
www.abooksmind.com

ISBN 978-1-939828-94-1

CONTENTS

FOREWORD
BY DR. BILL HAMON

Paul Renfroe has done an excellent job of enlightening and enabling Christians to see mankind and life as God sees them.

Those who are interested in having the mind of Christ will love this book. The scriptures Paul uses help to remove the blindfolds of human opinion that is contrary to God's way of thinking! God's number one priority for every Christian is for each one to be conformed to the image of Jesus Christ (Rom. 8:29, 1Cor. 3:18). Most Christians rejoice in Rev. 5:10 which reveal that the saints are to rule and reign with Christ.

However there will be no Christians in that ruling and reigning group who has not learned to think, act and judge according to God's righteous nature. That is one reason this book is so vital for the Body of Christ.

This book will remove the blindfolds that keep us from God's way of thinking and God's way for judging all things! All of our Christian experiences are "Training for Reigning, Schooling for Ruling and Maturing for Ministry." This book will help you prepare to be a joint heir with Jesus Christ.

God bless you Paul, for allowing God to teach you these truths and now to share them with the rest of the Body of Christ.

Apostle/Dr. Bill Hamon

Bishop: Christian International Ministries Network (CIMN),
              Christian International Apostolic Network (CIAN)
              Christian International Global Network (CIGN)

Author: Twelve major books on Apostolic and Prophetic such
              as *Prophets and Personal Prophecy.*

WELCOME

Why have you begun this book? Did the title intrigue you? Did someone recommend it to you? They may have spoken of the effect it had on their lives, an effect you want in yours.

Look past these visible causes, to the unseen reason you have begun this book. Look to Jesus Christ, the Lord of every Christian, submitted or not. It was He who put this book in your hand. He is bringing you to greater faith in biblical truths, truths of what God says you are.

Please focus your primary attention on the basic idea, the essential report this book is making to you, namely: you are a living spirit, able to function as a spirit.

Before proceeding further, look inward to your own heart.

- ☑ Can you receive a fresh new unfolding and unveiling of spiritual truth from the Bible?
- ☑ Can you accept that He keeps things hidden in the Bible until we are ready?
- ☑ Is your heart open to God teaching you what you have never seen before?
- ☑ Can you move into further knowledge that only God can enable you to have?
- ☑ Can you gain new comprehension of God's biblical revelations?

Yes? Then this may be your first new thought: eternity will be different because of you. That is how prominent you are in His plans—the subject of this workbook.

I asked you to check your inward responses. Knowing your heart helps you overcome inward resistance when you begin fully perceiving biblical truths about yourself. The Apostle Paul wrote in Romans 8:7 and I Corinthians 2:14,

the sinful mind is hostile to God. It does not submit to God's law, nor can it do so....The man without the Spirit does not accept the things that come from the Spirit of God, for they are foolishness to him, and he cannot understand them, because they are spiritually discerned.

This hostility is aroused when we have wrong, half-true or bad ideas in us. Such ideas function as blindfolds, protecting our sinful mind from the full perception of biblical truth.

People including Christians have bad ideas all the time. It's part of the normal course of life. Some are easy to correct, and some resist it. For instance, when people become Christians, many bad ideas are quickly laid to rest, such as "I am Lord of my own life." There are also bad political ideas and bad business ideas, bad ideas in every area of life which are often changed by undeniable circumstances.

So you can relax and look at your own thinking without fear. Truly, it would be unusual for you *not* to have wrong and half-true ideas.

To me, the hardest bad ideas to correct are the ones you have about yourself. While you read this book, those are the ideas which will put up a fight. That's normal. Simply consider the Scriptures presented. Fight for your elevation, fight for the revealing of who you really are—by assertively yielding to the Scripture. It will pierce you to the division of your soul & spirit; before it you have no secrets (Hebrews 4:12-13).

No secrets! That might make your heart nervous even though your mind agrees that God sees all. Assertively yielding to Scripture enables you to ditch those old limits and to become free from wrong thinking about yourself and God. That's why Jesus said in John 8:32,

You shall know the truth, and the truth shall set you free.

Imagine being a mighty warrior. You're fully equipped to dominate every enemy and humiliate every attacker. Now imagine you are blindfolded and don't know you are a mighty warrior. Unable to see, you would be uncertain, unnerved by noise, and even cowering. You can't even pick up your mighty weapons lying close at hand. This book is for removing that blindfold so you can see and be what you are according to the Scripture. That is freedom.

Contained in each chapter are activation exercises. These are things for you to do. A pen is *definitely* required for you to benefit fully. In James 1:22-24 God says,

> *Do not merely listen to the word, and so deceive yourselves. Do what it says. Anyone who listens to the word but does not do what it says is like a man who looks at his face in a mirror and, after looking at himself, goes away and immediately forgets what he looks like.*

Bishop Bill Hamon can be thanked for applying the simple concept of activation to the Christian life: "The word 'activate' means to make active or operative. It takes something from an inactive state and causes it to become functional." (Dr. Bill Hamon, *70 Reasons for Speaking in Tongues*, Parsons Publishing House, 2010, p. 86)

Do not bring judgment upon yourself by just absorbing facts and doing nothing with them. Hebrews 4:2 tells of accountability to add the actions of faith to the revelations God gives us from His Word:

> *the message they heard was of no value to them, because those who heard did not combine it with faith.*

Don't let that be you, dear friend! Instead, be like Paul who said, *with that same spirit of faith, we also believe and therefore speak.*

(II Corinthians 4:13) Remember, something in us resists truth. The activations help you to overcome that resistance so you can enjoy the truth as it sinks in.

Some activations simply ask you to check ☐Agree or ☐Disagree. Check your choice. You will be asked to review them, just for yourself, when you get to the later chapters.

Other activations are jotting down your answers to simple self-evaluations. Write them down. The physical act of writing gets your body involved and makes it an action of faith. Likewise, get your body involved with motion-oriented activation exercises also.

There are vocal activations. Speak it out aloud! Shout it if you can! Don't think of yourself as foolish. What you speak with your mouth is actually made invisibly real as your words speak it (one of the surprises awaiting you in this book). And words you speak either reinforce the bad ideas you have, or they defeat those bad ideas. So in this workbook, you will defeat them by actually speaking the biblical truths you see.

Besides, was not the world itself created by words? Did not God communicate to you in words? And your words signify what is in your heart—not by accident did Jesus say in Matthew 12:34, *For out of the overflow of the heart the mouth speaks.* So for your own sake, do the vocal activations as if your heart were full of God Almighty.

As a matter of fact, what do you know! the Scripture *does* teach, your heart *is* full of God Almighty.

Our introduction closes with this question for you. Jesus says in Matthew 11:12,

The kingdom of heaven is forcefully advancing, and forceful men lay hold of it.

Are you forcefully laying hold of it? If yes, you will relish this workbook. If no, maybe God will give you opportunity to do so in the future. Maybe, maybe not.

Because the kingdom of heaven is definitely advancing--with, or without, you. And that's a choice God Almighty has given to you as an honor.

God, please remove my blindfolds.

INTRODUCTION

Got your pen? You'll need it! Where you see Agree or Disagree, please choose one.

My calling in this workbook is to help you believe, receive, and activate what God revealed about you in the Bible—in short, to be what you are, Christian, to be a functioning spirit.

At present, you may not believe what you are. You may not even know what you are, for God has only recently allowed understanding to be unfolded from Scripture to large numbers of Christians.

With that, I have assumed a truth which may be new to you and which you can weigh for yourself in this introduction. Allow me to call it to your attention. We will also establish, with your pen, the agreements you and I have on basic Christian truths.

Deuteronomy 29:29 is a handy verse to help us recognize our limits and freedoms with God's revelations: *The secret things belong to the LORD our God, but the things revealed belong to us and to our children forever.*

I believe we can only receive revelation that God intends to give.
❏Agree ❏Disagree

I believe the Holy Bible is God's final self-revelation, is authoritative and is complete.
❏Agree ❏Disagree

I believe Jesus Christ died for our salvation, He rose from the dead, He poured out the promised Holy Spirit upon His followers, and worshiping Him with other Christians is of equal importance to Him as our walking with Him individually.
❏Agree ❏Disagree

Now for the truth I assumed above: although the Scriptures contain everything God means us to know about Him and the faith

He has called us to, we Christians as a body have not had the maturity to receive all that is in it.

❏Agree ❏Disagree

In other words, God Himself has allowed His church to develop and mature over time, and has opened our eyes to truths in Scripture at times He felt we were ready.

❏Agree ❏Disagree

You could well question this. After all, the Bible is composed of words on paper. How hard can it be to understand if someone has a willing heart? Yet witness in Scripture how frequently He Himself participates in someone not understanding.

The disciples themselves were front and center to history's greatest shift, history's greatest man, and history's greatest deed. Nonetheless, in Mark 8:14-21 is one of many passages showing how little they got it! Their capacity to understand what they were seeing was under-developed. Jesus calls attention to it with the words I underlined.

The disciples had forgotten to bring bread, except for one loaf they had with them in the boat. "Be careful," Jesus warned them. "Watch out for the yeast of the Pharisees and that of Herod."

They discussed this with one another and said, "It is because we have no bread."

Aware of their discussion, Jesus asked them: "Why are you talking about having no bread? <u>Do you still not see or understand? Are your hearts hardened? Do you have eyes but fail to see, and ears but fail to hear?</u> And don't you remember? When I broke the five loaves for the five thousand, how many basketsful of pieces did you pick up?"

"Twelve," they replied.

"And when I broke the seven loaves for the four thousand, how many basketsful of pieces did you pick up?"

They answered, "Seven."

He said to them, "<u>Do you still not understand?</u>"

Luke 9:45 describes a hiding of the truth from the disciples which God clearly participated in.

But they did not understand what this meant. It was hidden from them, so that they did not grasp it, and they were afraid to ask him about it.

Jesus himself participated in preventing recognition. Consider the road to Emmaus (Luke 24:15-16):

As they talked and discussed these things with each other, Jesus himself came up and walked along with them; but they were kept from recognizing him.

Advance to one of several great unveilings in church history—1517. The discoveries made by Martin Luther and the other reformers had been in the Bible all along. They used the Latin standard Bible known as the Vulgate which was then 1,100 years old, and the key Reformation truths from Habakkuk 2:4 and Romans 1:16-17 were in the Bible all those years, just like they are today.

In fact, church history shows that prior to 1517 many Christians had come to perceive these truths in the Bible. During that period, it had been received by individuals (both clergy and laymen), but not by the Church as a whole. So these Christians who were so blessed, either isolated themselves into the monasteries or were persecuted by the resistive religious authorities. Anthony (died 356 AD) was known for his spiritual perception, and was the first of many to live apart in what later became the monastic movement. Madame Guyon (died 1717) exemplified those who remained engaged with the church at large, despite being persecuted by its religious authorities for her spiritual perception.

You can further explore this understanding of church history as our maturation process. One excellent book is *The Eternal Church* by Dr. Bill Hamon, founder and Bishop of Christian International Ministries. (Shippensburg PA: Destiny Image Publishers, 2003)

For your workbook, can you agree His Church matures over time?

❏Agree ❏Disagree

Can you agree that at His chosen times, God brings to our awareness Scriptural truths never absent, yet never widely perceived?

❏Agree ❏Disagree

If so, then you will find in this book biblical truths that make sense of many loose ends you have lived with. What follows this introduction will introduce you to freedom you never dreamt existed. Say goodbye to your blindfold.

Before commencing the workbook, my testimony will address your curiosity about me as the author. My wife and I are well-educated and have a well-versed background. People know us as lifelong learners.

We served full-time in a leading national ministry for 12 years. Many Christians have been nurtured and sent out under our ministry both then and since. We have led at every level of church except pastor. We have received teaching of globally recognized quality and have been well-grounded in the Scripture all our adult lives.

Yet, we too have experienced the hiding of Scriptural truths as God awaited our readiness. For 30 years we didn't have the maturity to perceive in Scripture what you are about to read in this book!

In 2006 we began to experience things in our walk with Jesus that surprised us. As we studied the Scripture about it, we perceived these things there plainly—verses we had been reading without understanding for years.

We also found that we had no one in our Christian circle who could explain to us either what we were perceiving or what we were experiencing. As our blindfolds came off, some didn't know what to make of us.

Could that be you as well?

You might wonder about my background, or the ministry I refer to—or what tradition has influenced me. The Apostle Paul had a response I have always liked, in II Corinthians 12:6:

> *I refrain [from discussing myself], so no one will think more of me than is warranted by what I do or say.*

With your permission, I ask you to judge the following content on its own merits, by its basis in and explanation of Scripture, rather than by my background.

However, to help you resist pigeonholing the contents of this book, with my denominational background and church memberships, I have been called a

"MethoBapTerIcAliaCostal."

Does that help some?

CHAPTER 1:
ARE YOU A CHRISTIAN?

So you are a Christian. What is that?

You might feel very comfortable that you know the answer. But will you ponder it slowly with me? This will help you benefit more fully in coming chapters.

First we'll consider how people you know define a Christian. Then we'll look at your own definition and God's, too. This should be affirming for you. At the same time you may see some infectious half-truths that our general culture has promoted to blindfold you. If that happens, you may feel uncomfortable but I encourage you, keep going! There's freedom on the other side.

So begin with this activation—to understand how people you know define a Christian. Put a friend's name in the first blank of the sentence below, your name in the second, and finish it with something you think that friend would say. Be sure to include the thoughts of your possibly unsaved friends.

ACTIVATION 1-1

"_____ (friend's name)

thinks _____ (your name) is definitely a

Christian because _____

_____."

What have you placed in the last blank? Using a variety of friends, acquaintances and family members in the first blank, write down below what you think they would say in the last blank.

1. name _____

would say _____

2. name _____

would say _____

3. name _____

would say _____

4. name _____

would say _____

5. name _____

would say _____

Now please remember: that activation was about popular beliefs of what a Christian is. Let's turn to what you think. Please write your own answers now to this one:

ACTIVATION 1-2

"I am a Christian & that means I _____."

1. _____

2. _____

3. _____

4. _____

5. _____

Now I imagine that the things you just wrote are probably good things! I doubt you just wrote down, "I am a Christian and that means I hate everybody."

There is a third question to consider, and for your benefit only, write down your answers.

ACTIVATION 1-3

"What is a Christian changed into, after becoming a Christian?"

1. _____

2. _____

3. _____

4. _____

5. _____

The point of those activations was to see how people you know and you define "Christian." Your answers above will also help you for the rest of this book. They will give you a benchmark for where you are now.

The $20,000 question of course is this: What does God consider a Christian to be?

It may surprise you the Bible doesn't answer that question. The word "Christian' is used only three times in the Bible, beginning with Acts 11:26: *The disciples were called Christians first at Antioch.* Not once is it used by Jesus.

We can get at the same answer though—with a different question. "What satisfied Jesus Christ that someone believed Him?"

Does that seem like a fair rewording to you? I like it because it calls attention to *His* evaluation, whereas the word "Christian" is more weighted to other people's assessment of us. Since Jesus, not other people, is Judge on Judgment Day, I am a lot more interested in His evaluation than theirs.

What *did* satisfy Jesus that someone believed in Him? He sure made it plain what did *not* satisfy Him. Let's start with that.

For instance, many people think a Christian is someone who believes in Jesus. But the way we mean "believes" cannot be what Jesus meant. Jesus was cautious toward many people who believed in him. Apostle John records this in John 2:23-25--

Now while he was in Jerusalem at the Passover Feast, many people saw the miraculous signs he was doing and believed in his name. But Jesus would not entrust himself to them, for he knew all men. He did not need man's testimony about man, for he knew what was in a man.

Jesus repeatedly revealed a low regard for people merely believing in Him. In Luke 6:46, He says to people who clamored for Him, *Why do you call me 'Lord, Lord,' and do not do what I say?* Today our term for this is, "lip service." He expresses this low regard again in a shocking way in Matthew 7:21-23 (speaking of Judgment Day!):

Not everyone who says to me, 'Lord, Lord,' will enter the kingdom of heaven, but only he who does the will of my Father who is in heaven. Many will say to me on that day, 'Lord, Lord, did we not prophesy in your name, and in your name drive out demons and perform many miracles?' Then I will tell them plainly, 'I never knew you. Away from me, you evildoers!'

I don't know about you, but I consider that an impressive list of Christian accomplishments and displays of power. Don't you think these people would be considered *strong* Christians in your church?

In all religious groups, standards arise for ideal behavior. Take a moment to make a list here of everything a Christian is supposed to do—in popular opinion, or in preaching you have heard.

ACTIVATION 1-4

1. _____
2. _____
3. _____
4. _____
5. _____

As with activation 1-2, I am certain you listed good things, actions founded on righteous desires. So did the rich young ruler, in Luke 18:18-23.

A certain ruler asked him, "Good teacher, what must I do to inherit eternal life?"

"Why do you call me good?" Jesus answered. "No one is good—except God alone. You know the commandments: 'Do not commit adultery, do not murder, do not steal, do not give false testimony, honor your father and mother.'"

"All these I have kept since I was a boy," he said.

When Jesus heard this, he said to him, "You still lack one thing. Sell everything you have and give to the poor, and you will have treasure in heaven. Then come, follow me."

We see that Jesus didn't put as high a priority on behavior standards as on following Him. Predictably, the leaders who prized conformity to religious behaviors criticized Him. That's why, in Mark 7:6-7, He applied Isaiah 29:13 to those religious leaders:

Isaiah was right when he prophesied about you hypocrites; as it is written:

The Lord says: "These people come near to me with their mouth and honor me with their lips, but their hearts are far from me. Their worship of me is made up only of rules taught by men."

By now, your half-truths and bad ideas might be rebelling against what you have just read from the Scripture. Is Jesus really saying that obeying the Ten Commandments didn't satisfy Him? That worshiping Him in praise didn't satisfy Him? That miracle-working didn't satisfy Him?

Looks like He is really saying that. But accept the Father's mercy; and have His mercy on those who taught you as best they could. It is God who decides when, how and to whom to release the truths in His Word.

So far we still have our question: "What satisfied Jesus Christ that someone believed Him? What *did* He want them to do? What *does* He want you and me to do?"

Because the people face to face with Him were not ready for it, He used stories, parables to help them understand. Such as the one about children in Matthew 18:3—

I tell you the truth, unless you change and become like little children, you will never enter the kingdom of heaven.

We often hear this quoted. What is it about a child which, if present in you, satisfies Jesus? Clearly not miracle working like the people He described on Judgment Day—although He is obviously not against miracle working. Children are trusting, yielding, weak, submissive to authority, loving, wanting, incapable, teachable. Are you?

He also used farming parables such as in Mark 4:1-20, usually called the parable of the sower when it is actually about the soils. There He concludes in verse 20,

Others, like seed sown on good soil, hear the word, accept it, and produce a crop—thirty, sixty or even a hundred times what was sown.

Are you good soil?

Money parables were frequent too. In the parable of the talents, Jesus was represented by the Master who evaluated the performance of three servants. What did He say in Matthew 25:21 & 23 to those who satisfied Him?

Well done, good and faithful servant! You have been faithful with a few things; I will put you in charge of many things. Come and share your master's happiness!

Are you being faithful with the few things He has put in your life?

The toughest parables He used involved the cross, such as Luke 9:23-27 below. Remember this: his hearers did not know He would die on a cross. They knew it exclusively as you and I know an electric chair, gas chamber or gallows—a terrible way criminals are put to death.

If anyone would come after me, he must deny himself and take up his cross daily and follow me. For whoever wants to save his life will lose it, but whoever loses his life for me will save it.

What would you think about a teacher who told you that to be associated with Him, you had to come with Him to the electric chair? Maybe that's why there were only 12 disciples. Yet Jesus used this language on purpose and repeatedly. Why?

Jesus was satisfied when people *followed* Him. He was *not* satisfied simply when they believed some facts about Him, or wanted to be around Him, or to have His blessings, or to wield His powers. He was satisfied in followers who would pay the cost—even if it meant death.

In Luke 9:57-62, we read of three people whom He did not accept, because of their responses. (Dietrich Bonhoeffer's life-changing exposition of these incidents can be found in his book, *The Cost of Discipleship*, New York: Macmillan, 1966.)

A man said to him, "I will follow you wherever you go." Jesus replied, "Foxes have holes and birds of the air have nests, but the Son of Man has no place to lay his head." He said to another man, "Follow me." But the man replied, "Lord, first let me go and bury my father." Jesus said to him, "Let the dead bury their own dead, but you go and proclaim the kingdom of God." Still another said, "I will follow you, Lord; but first let me go back and say good-by to my family." Jesus replied, "No one who puts his hand to the plow and looks back is fit for service in the kingdom of God."

As you see, Jesus clearly expected them to say goodbye to what we consider normal life expectations and desires. He did not have low standards for followers. He expected full and sole obedience at the same time we are childlike.

Jesus wasn't negative or constantly judging, as we are about to see. He taught that being His follower qualified you for lofty, exalting truths—far higher than you dare to imagine. These include teachings further developed in the New Testament, as the Holy Spirit inspired the apostles.

He also knows our frame, and that it takes time for us to grow. However, He certainly did not tolerate people taking refuge in one religious behavior or another, as if they were finished following. He requires believers who are followers. And that is a circle He drew clearly. He Himself said, *Many are called but few are chosen.* (Matthew 22:14)

ACTIVATION 1-5

Above are several Scriptures about us Christians. Review them one by one and review your benchmark answers in activations 1-1 through 1-4. Compare your answers to the Scriptures.

My answers matched	Scriptures	I was corrected
	Jn 2:23-24 (BELIEF)	
	Mt 7:21-23 (POWER)	
	Lk 18:18-23 (GOOD DEEDS)	
	Is. 29:13 (WORSHIP)	
	Mt 18:3 (CHILDLIKE)	
	Mk 4:20 (REPRODUCTIVE)	
	Mt 25:21,23 (FAITHFUL)	
	Lk 9:23-27 (SELF-SACRIFICE)	
	Lk 9:57-62 (FORSAKING ALL)	

I am willing to be corrected by Scripture.
☐Agree ☐Disagree

ACTIVATION 1-6

This is another benchmarking activation you will refer back to. Write down brief thoughts on these questions. (Ignore the M & D for now; we will use them when we look back at this.)

☐ M ☐ D Why did Jesus want a church?

❒ M ❒ D What is the church for?

_____

_____

❒ M ❒ D Why bother with the church when it is so much trouble?

_____

_____

❒ M ❒ D What is the Gospel for, anyway?

_____

_____

❒ M ❒ D What is a Christian supposed to do?

_____

_____

In activations 1-1 through 1-5, you listed many ideas about what a Christian is, and compared it with what Jesus said about His followers. Another valuable comparison is our popular understanding of Christianity with what is emphasized in the Bible. And since Christianity is not a Bible term, we'll look at the gospel Jesus preached.

His death on the cross for sin and our salvation by faith were included in His gospel. Up until now these (and going to church) have formed the limit of many people's understanding. But by volume, by sheer amount of words, His statements on those subjects are far fewer than other topics. He didn't say much about why He would die or about our salvation. He didn't say much about church, and used the word "church" only 2 times. It's a surprising contrast to our practice of Christianity.

Fortunately the Gospel writers summarized His preaching for us, as in Mark 1:14-15--

Jesus went into Galilee, proclaiming the good news of God. "The time has come," He said. "The kingdom of God is near. Repent and believe the good news."

The apostles wrote that Jesus' gospel preaching was about the Kingdom of God. It's a short summary. His preaching was *not* about the pragmatic steps we have to go through to get into it.

That's a challenge for us. The pragmatic steps for getting in and staying in is where our "checklist" focus lies. That focus is why we reduce Christianity to "do's and don'ts." This checklist focus acts as a blindfold, obscuring what we are. As good as your earlier activation answers were, are they not just more "do's and don'ts?"

At our time in history, God is now releasing for our perception, world-wide and *en masse*, what has been in Scripture all along but little perceived. His desire is not for saved souls who can stick to a list of "do's and don'ts." His longing is for a Kingdom where His voice is heard and obeyed by those saved souls. He has the Groom's longing for a many-membered Church (composed of those saved souls) to be His Bride, His Army, and to reign in life as well as eternally on the new earth! That was what Hebrews 12:2 calls *the joy set before him.* Here are Scriptures that are waking people up in this matter.

Then the sovereignty, power and greatness of the kingdoms under the whole heaven will be handed over to the saints, the people of the most High. (Daniel 7:27)

I will build My church...Whatever you bind on earth will be bound in heaven. Whatever you loose on earth will be loosed in heaven. (Matthew 16:18)

And I confer on you a kingdom, just as my Father conferred one on Me, so that you may eat and drink at My table in My Kingdom and sit on thrones, judging the twelve tribes of Israel. (Luke 22:29)

I have given you authority to trample on snakes and scorpions and to overcome all the power of the enemy; nothing will harm you. (Luke 10:19)

How much more will [the saints] reign in life through the one man, Jesus Christ! (Romans 5:17)

Do you not know that the saints will judge the world? (I Corinthians 6:2)

You have made them to be a kingdom and priests to serve our God and they will reign on the earth. (Revelation 5:10)

Then I saw a new heaven and a new earth, for the first heaven and the first earth had passed away, and there was no longer any sea. I saw the Holy City, the new Jerusalem, coming down out of heaven from God, prepared as a bride beautifully dressed for her husband. (Revelation 21:1-2)

ACTIVATION 1-7

Look back at your ideas of what Church is for and there check ❑M for your answers that matched with Jesus' statements above, and ❑D for your answers that differed from the above. Limit your comparison just to the above Scriptures.

ACTIVATION 1-8

Write out your comparison of your answers in 1-6 and the Scriptures above.

My answers	question	Scriptures above
	WHY JESUS WANTS CHURCH	
	WHAT CHURCH IS FOR	
	WHY BOTHER?	
	WHAT GOSPEL IS FOR	
	WHAT A C'TN IS SUPPOSED TO DO	

Can you believe the gospel that Jesus had in mind when He preached it? Can you accept the highly important place He intends for you? After all, what follows in this book is only available on Jesus' terms. He is the Judge. Are you following Him?

If so, this workbook is devoted to the characteristics which Scripture reveals that you have as Jesus' follower. Please note that these characteristics are manifested gradually; Scripture doesn't say it happens overnight. That doesn't change the truth about you which is plainly stated in the Word of God.

ACTIVATION 1-9

Please read the following list aloud! (Disregard the blanks for now.)

_____ I have spiritual perception, enabling me to sense heavenly realities. (Chapter 2)

_____ I am God's beloved child, His named beneficiary though completely undeserving, and object of His favor. (3)

_____ I am one of a new race of men, due to the depth of my spiritual transformation. (4)

_____ I am a spirit-dominant creature and I receive my most essential sustenance through my spirit, not my body. (5)

_____ I am a creature who now has continual communion and rest with my Creator. (6)

_____ I am a fully equipped ruler, ruling by my will and my words, and my rulership awaits my maturing into it. (7)

_____ I am an essential expression of God's love and a minister contributing to the maturing of Christ's eternal bride, the Church. (8)

_____ I am a sign and evidence of the age to come, a conviction to people around me, preparing them for God to reveal Himself to them. (9)

_____ I am an Earth-ruler and physical reality is ready to respond to me and to God in me. (10)

_____ I am a fearsome opponent & undefeatable conqueror of God's enemies, & we are their fearsome replacement. (11)

_____ I am my Father's child. (Epilogue)

These will be amply demonstrated to be true of you, Christian, from God's own words about you.

ACTIVATION 1-10

Did you read the list *aloud*? Read it again, a second time, but this time, imagine you are notifying a large resistant crowd of your position and authority in their midst. (That probably involves standing up on something to get higher, don't you suppose? Act the part!)

ACTIVATION 1-11

Now in the blanks by each identity statement in activation 1-9, please rank them according to your comfort with them, as of this reading. On a scale of 1 to 10, use 1 for most comfortable and 10 for least. 5 might mean "not sure" or "depends on the situation."

Lastly, consider—the members of the Church described in Scripture: could they be any less than the above? For God to ask what He does of us, to appoint us to such pre-eminent responsibilities— could we be any less than the above? To receive the kingdom, to reign in life, doesn't there have to be more to you than you see right now?

Could it be possible that God asks *you* to do what looks impossible because His living in you *actually* makes you able? Not just in thought or doctrine only, but *in actual fact*? Possible that we don't seem able because we are blindfolded from seeing what we are? Let's see.

Father, I want to let go of my blindfolds. Please help me!

CHAPTER 2:
NO MORE BLINDFOLD: YOU ARE A SPIRITUALLY PERCEPTIVE CREATURE

A common element in the truths of the last chapter is the capability of spiritual perception which you receive as a Christian. The Apostle John makes this so plain in I John 2:12-21 & 26-27, which are hard to grasp unless you understand that you have spiritual perception as a child of God:

> *But you have an anointing from the Holy One, and all of you know the truth. I do not write to you because you do not know the truth, but because you do know it and because no lie comes from the truth.... As for you, the anointing you received from him remains in you, and you do not need anyone to teach you. But as His anointing teaches you about all things and as that anointing is real, not counterfeit—just as it has taught you, remain in Him.*

Perception is *like* your five senses, but more. Perception is *not* about the pathway through which you perceive something. It's about the resulting awareness. Whereas seeing is about eyes, and hearing is about ears, perception is about awareness—the result. This is why Jesus distinguishes spiritual perception from natural, in Mark 4:11, as He quotes Isaiah 6:9-10.

> *to those on the outside everything is said in parables so that, 'they may be ever seeing but never perceiving, and ever hearing but never understanding...'*

This distinction between spiritual perception and natural perception explains why this statement of Jesus was recorded 17 times: *he who has ears to hear, let him hear.* (Mark 4:9) Jesus wasn't speaking to ear amputees. He perceived that some are content not to have spiritual perception, to be blindfolded.

ACTIVATION 2-1

Let's begin with an activating study in Scripture. Below are Mark 9:2-9, the Transfiguration, and Revelation 1:14-16, where John sees Jesus after His ascension. In the chart afterward, write down the physical elements of Jesus' appearance in each.

Mark 9:2-9 After six days Jesus took Peter, James and John with him and led them up a high mountain, where they were all alone. There he was transfigured before them. His clothes became dazzling white, whiter than anyone in the world could bleach them. And there appeared before them Elijah and Moses, who were talking with Jesus.

Peter said to Jesus, "Rabbi, it is good for us to be here. Let us put up three shelters—one for you, one for Moses and one for Elijah." (He did not know what to say, they were so frightened.)

Then a cloud appeared and enveloped them, and a voice came from the cloud: "This is my Son, whom I love. Listen to him!"

Revelation 1:12-17 I turned around to see the voice that was speaking to me. And when I turned I saw seven golden lampstands, and among the lampstands was someone "like a son of man," dressed in a robe reaching down to his feet and with a golden sash around his chest. His head and hair were white like wool, as white as snow, and his eyes were like blazing fire. His feet were like bronze glowing in a furnace, and his voice was like the sound of rushing waters. In his right hand he held seven stars, and out of his mouth came a sharp double-edged sword. His face was like the sun shining in all its brilliance.

When I saw him, I fell at his feet as though dead.

Mark 9:3-4	Revelation 1:14-16

In the Transfiguration, it wasn't some magic show or dramatization they witnessed. The eyes of the disciples were momentarily opened. They perceived what Revelation 1:14-16 displays as Jesus' permanent and unchanging glory. The variable was the perception permitted to them. This variation of perception is evident all across peoples' responses to Jesus.

Paul writes in Ephesians of Christians being equipped. In 5:8-14 the equipment of spiritual perception is described as a functioning capacity for light, a capacity that we did not have before.

For you were once darkness, but now you are light in the Lord. Live as children of light (for the fruit of the light consists in all goodness, righteousness and truth) and find out what pleases the Lord. Have nothing to do with the fruitless deeds of darkness, but rather expose them. For it is shameful even to mention what the disobedient do in secret. But everything exposed by the light becomes visible, for it is light that makes everything visible. This is why it is said:

"Wake up, O sleeper, rise from the dead, and Christ will shine on you."

1. **Biblical perception concerns objective truth**. A caution is necessary due to our modern usage, using the word "perception" to scorn truth, or to describe someone's inaccurate grasp of reality. It is also used to justify the idea that truth differs among people according to their viewpoint. People use the word "perception" to support their rationalizations of their behaviors also.

Not here! The biblical concept of perception is of truth, and nothing but the truth. The foremost embodiment of the truth is the Scripture and so our spiritual perception is entirely founded on the Scripture. Any spiritual perception that is not founded on Scripture may be accurate but it is counterfeit, not true, perception.

2. **Spiritual perception results in an awareness of the unseen**. The Bible teaches us that the most real reality includes the unseen world, and that the visible reality is dominated by the unseen reality. When the blindfold comes off, the new awareness in you pierces and transforms. Instead of being more information, this awareness puts your seen life into the context of the unseen surrounding you.

This is why Apostle Paul writes in II Corinthians 4:18,

So we fix our eyes not on what is seen, but on what is unseen.
For what is seen is temporary, but what is unseen is eternal.

3. **Spiritual perception focuses on God Himself**. Psalm 25 is a pre-eminent description of spiritual perception and accordingly it begins, *To you, O LORD, I lift up my soul.* The more we gaze at Him and yield our attention to Him, He releases more perception to us, He *confides* in us. This is experienced as becoming aware, having impressions, or as often described, "feeling led."

The event of becoming aware is described in Scripture as having your eyes opened, or your mind opened to heavenly reality. We touched on the two Emmaus disciples becoming aware in Luke 24:31--*"Then their eyes were opened and they recognized Him."*

Mark 11:23 is often cited about faith that moves mountains, to build our faith that prayer is answered. But the context in 11:22 cannot be neglected: *"Have faith in God,"* Jesus answered. How can so much teaching skip over that verse? This is a warning that the focus might be on God's things, rather than on God. To settle for God's things when God offers Himself is cowering, blindfolded behavior. Answered prayer is good, but it's nothing compared to ditching the blindfold and knowing God. This is what Paul meant in Philippians 3: 7-8 after describing his life of religious fulfillment:

> But whatever was to my profit I now consider loss for the sake of Christ. What is more, I consider everything a loss compared to the surpassing greatness of knowing Christ Jesus my Lord, for whose sake I have lost all things. I consider them rubbish, that I may gain Christ

Blindness to God can result from a focus on God's things, as it did for the Jewish leaders of Jesus' day. Be sure you don't leave out the most important teaching—focus on God. A similar error was indulged by the recipients of the letter to the Hebrews, who began to focus on angels at cost of their focus on Jesus. Hebrews 1-2 is focused on its correction.

4. **Spiritual perception is how we know what pleases God**. In Ephesians 5:10 cited above, we are told to *find out what pleases the Lord*. Jesus said to his critics in John 8:29, *The one who sent me is with me; he has not left me alone, for I always do what pleases him.* He gave you spiritual perception so you could know what pleases Him in any given moment.

The Scripture doesn't address every situation of daily life but reveals who God is and His principles for life. Founded on the truth of Scripture, you can perceive His heart and mind in most of life's daily situations.

God said what He wanted in His servant in I Samuel 2:35, and it requires spiritual perception.

> I will raise up for Myself a faithful priest who will do according to what is on My heart and mind.

5. **The heavenly reality of which we become aware is real whether people perceive it or not**. We have for example

the unbelievably beautiful galaxies and star-fields captured on film by the Hubble space telescope. Were they less real or less beautiful because until now people had never seen them?

Before angels appeared to the shepherds tending their sheep on a Bethlehem hillside, was God's glory around them? Yes it was, for as Scripture tells us in Isaiah 6:3, *The whole earth is full of His glory.* But the shepherds only became aware of it at His will, when first one and then a host of angels appeared, each in their turn. (Luke 2:9,13) Is His glory around you right now? Yes, ready to be perceived.

Elisha taught this to his servant in II Kings 6, namely, that we are not the only entities present. Many beings may be present at any time. With our perceptive capacity from God, we can also see that we are the most *exalted* ones present, as Scripture plainly teaches. Whether our blindfold is gone or not, we are still what Scripture says we are.

And in every moment we can be aware of spiritual resources not perceptible to others. This is one thing Jesus meant when He told His disciples in John 4:34, *I have food to eat which you know nothing about.*

A reader would do well to ask, "Apostle Paul, how do I fix my eyes on something I cannot see? If I know nothing about something, how do I perceive it?"

6. **Spiritual perception follows faith**. We accept a statement of God in the Scripture, and that faith-acceptance activates our perception of the heavenly reality. Faith matures from mental agreement with facts and propositions, to certainty and reliance upon the God we know. Spiritual perception also matures alongside faith.

Example: you accept God's statement that your sins are forgiven when you believe in Jesus and His death for your sin. This is a faith-based acceptance that an unseen fact is true. So from the very beginning, you have relied by faith upon unseen truths. Yet despite this faith, when you sin, and even after confession and repenting, inward condemnation can still plague your heart. You cry out to God and the Holy Spirit helps you overcome this condemnation. Eventually you become *aware* that you really are forgiven. As you grow in that awareness, you quickly believe you are forgiven when you sin in the future. Faith grows, and spiritual perception follows it.

The classic verse on perception following faith is Hebrews 4:2-3 where the restful peace God wanted Israel to have is lost to them because

> *The message they heard was of no value to them, because they did not combine it with faith. Now we who have believed enter that rest....*

The faith Jesus commended in those who received miracles from him was not a doctrinal faith that consisted of points and subpoints. It was a faith that identified him as the man God sent to them with rulership over their situation. As seen in chapter 1, Jesus gave his contemporaries very little explanation of what we today call the gospel. They simply heard him teach that the kingdom of heaven was near, that he was bringing it, and they believed him.

7. **The perception of God and of activity in the heavenlies is not experienced mentally.** Spiritual perception is not subject to a scientific-level review of how you become aware. It isn't logical to any training based in the visible world. However, when you perceive something spiritually and receive it with faith, you perceive a logic in it that is higher and surpasses words and thoughts. The words "know" and "knowing" are about the only words we have to describe the certainty we gain from spiritually perceiving something, but that is not an indication that the process is mental or logical.

This perception of a higher logic is demonstrated in Luke 7:1-10, where a Roman centurion said a curious thing as Jesus approached his home to heal a sick servant. It's curious because it defied all natural logic. After all, the centurion was a commanding officer in the occupying army, and Jesus was a poor traveling rabbi. A general and a preacher.

Every natural logic we use in daily life says the preacher would be less prominent than the general and thus the less worthy of the two. Natural logic also would say, if you can be friends with a mighty miracle worker, do it. But the centurion of the occupying army felt himself the least worthy, and sent messengers to stop Jesus from coming, with this message in Luke 7:6-8:

> *Lord, don't trouble yourself, for I do not deserve to have you come under my roof. That is why I did not even consider myself worthy to come to you. But say the word, and my servant will be healed. For I myself am a man under authority, with soldiers under me. I tell this one, 'Go,' and he goes; and that one, 'Come,' and he comes. I say to my servant, 'Do this,' and he does it.*

The centurion perceived that Jesus commanded an unseen world, the world most influential over his servant's illness. He saw Jesus' authority was like his own authority to command inferior ranks. But he was aware that Jesus' authority was over the unseen, an authority of far higher rank than the centurion's. That's why the centurion didn't consider himself worthy of a visit from Jesus. Since the centurion also perceived that Jesus' command does not require physical proximity, and is not impaired by distance, he asked, *Merely say the word.*

8. Hebrews 4:2-3 above and similar Scriptures also teach us that **spiritual perception is not an ability we gain and hold onto**. Rather, it is a gift of God. His favor provides us with awareness of truths, realities, and entities, in His timing. He does not give spiritual perception to those who are not followers of Jesus nor could they obtain such perception even if they wanted to, as Paul writes in Romans 9:18, *"God hardens those he wants to harden."*

Even Apostle Peter showed us that spiritual perception is not a permanent ability, when he visited the Antioch church, a mixed church.. Think about Peter! He had the three-time vision of Acts 10 that Gentiles were to be accepted into the church as equals to the Jewish Christians. Yet Peter lost this clarity in Antioch and began ostracizing Gentile Christians. Apostle Paul tells of his confrontation with Apostle Peter over this in Galatians 2.

So if this can happen even to Apostle Peter, it is clear that spiritual maturity doesn't equate to the possession of permanent perceptive ability. This fact is evident also in Peter's response to the attitude of Simon Magnus in Acts 8, who had exactly the concept that spiritual power was an ability to be acquired—and was sternly rebuked by Peter.

Clearly then, spiritual perception is not an ability that we own, but rather, one we cultivate with daily attention to finding out what pleases the Lord.

9. **Spiritual perception can be imparted by one person to another**. Impartation occurs when a spiritual gift or capacity is given by one Christian to another. Elisha did this when he spoke to God about his servant in II Kings 6:17, *"O LORD, open his eyes, that he may see."* Paul prayed for the growing spiritual perception of others in Ephesians 1:17-18.

I keep asking that the God of our Lord Jesus Christ, the glorious Father, may give you the Spirit of wisdom and revelation, so that you may know him better. I pray also that the eyes of your heart may be enlightened in order that you may know the hope to which he has called you, the riches of his glorious inheritance in the saints, and his incomparably great power for us who believe.

Jesus imparted spiritual perception to his disciples in Luke 24:45—

Then he opened their minds so they could understand the Scriptures.

10. **Spiritual perception is a gift that we can cultivate and train**. Elijah presumed this when he told Elisha in II Kings 2:10, *"You have asked a difficult thing. Yet if you see me when I am taken from you, it will be yours—otherwise not."* Elisha is thereby invited to focus for perception of a spiritual event. It was a cultivation that benefited him later, as the events of II Kings 6 bear out.

Jesus frequently stated our responsibility for our spiritual perception: *"He who has an ear, let him hear."* Jesus uses this phrase in Matthew 11:15 and in 17 other places. In I Corinthians 14:32, Paul describes our personal responsibility for our perception and its expression: *"For the spirits of the prophets are subject to the control of the prophets."*

Hebrews 5:14 refers to a training process for your spiritual perception, which we might describe as trial and error: *"But solid food is for the mature, who by constant use have trained themselves to distinguish good from evil."* For such trial and error to occur, it helps to have an environment of love, safety and mutual trust, led by pastors & other good stewards of time and church life. In your own walk with God you can practice this trial-and-error learning.

11. **Speaking with our tongue is a valuable way to cultivate our spiritual perception**. As Paul wrote in Romans 10:10, *" with your heart you believe...and with your mouth you confess."* The activation in the previous chapter was to speak the list out loud about yourself. James writes about the power of the tongue in James 3:1-12. Paul presumed the predominance of *verbal* activity in I Corinthians 2:12-13, 14:4 & 14-15.

We have not received the spirit of the world but the Spirit who is from God, that we may understand what God has freely given us. This is what we speak, not in words taught by human wisdom but in words taught by the Spirit, expressing spiritual truths in spiritual words...He who speaks in a tongue edifies himself.... Anyone who speaks in a tongue should pray that he may interpret what he says. If I pray in a tongue, my spirit prays but my mind is unfruitful...I will pray with my spirit but I will also pray with my mind. I will sing with my spirit but I will also sing with my mind.

12. **Yielding your tongue to the Holy Spirit increases your awareness of spiritual things.** Yielding your tongue also includes speaking in tongues. This has been a subject of controversy in past years and thankfully that is largely behind. It is a resource for the Body of Christ, given by the Holy Spirit. Speaking in tongues is a very effective verbal activity for activating our spiritual perception—precisely because of the power of our tongue. It converts our speech to the purposes of the Holy Spirit.

Jude 20 says, *But you, dear friends, build yourselves up in your most holy faith and pray in the Holy Spirit.* Paul's chapter on spiritual warfare includes a similar admonition in Ephesians 6:18, *And pray in the Spirit on all occasions with all kinds of prayers and requests.*

It make sense that if God gives us spiritual perception as Jesus' followers, that He gives us spiritual communication also. Both capabilities are needed to be a functioning, living spirit. These abilities demonstrate that you are indeed a citizen of the Kingdom of the God who says this about Himself:

God is spirit, and his worshipers must worship in spirit and in truth. (John 4:24)

The most comprehensive teaching about speaking in tongues is I Corinthians chapter 12-14 where Apostle Paul did some problem-solving. The Corinthians abused love in their church events. This affected their speaking in tongues, as it did their Communion. We didn't abandon Communion on that basis, so likewise it's wrong to discount spiritual languages on that basis also. Sadly many Christians have thrown out the baby with the bathwater. To the contrary, Paul's response to their abuses strongly emphasizes the importance and benefit of speaking in tongues, as long as love governs.

Paul corrects the Corinthians' abuse specifically in church events, where something spoken to the Body at large in tongues will be interpreted. But when we relate individually to God, whether in private or with other worshipers harmoniously doing the same, interpretation into our natural language is not the expectation of I Corinthians 14 where Paul's guidance is given.

13. **Spiritual perception includes but is not limited to doctrine and teaching**. Jesus said to the woman at the well, *"the true worshipers will worship the Father in spirit and truth, for they are the kind of worshipers the Father seeks."* (John 4:23) Truth in doctrine is included as is truth in personal integrity, truth in spiritual communion, truth in spiritual perception and so forth.

Joel 2:28-29, cited by Peter on the day of Pentecost, clearly expands our perception past the limits of doctrine when it says we will *"dream dreams and see visions."* God intends for you to perceive the spiritual world more and more as you mature and grow.

Because spiritual perception isn't limited to doctrine and teaching, you don't have to have school training to have spiritual perception—just as no schooling is required to have a dream.

14. **How do you know whether you are perceiving something accurately**? The potential for inaccuracy has caused some leaders to disallow this biblical revelation of your spiritual perceptiveness. Fear of being inaccurate has been used to shut many Christians up and blindfold them. As Paul made plain to the Corinthians, love overcomes these things. Love creates the safe environment of mutual trust in a church body, and a protocol for trial and error.

The teaching of I John 2 above about your anointing is reassuring. But the point here is this: God doesn't deal with you based on the accuracy of your spiritual perception. He is moved by your submission to His process of developing you, which Hebrews emphasizes. That's why the trial-and-error process is described in Hebrews 5:14. That's why Hebrews 12:10 says that God's fathering you results in your sharing in His holiness.

This process consists of innumerable opportunities in daily life to believe Him obediently and to yield to your Father's trustworthy reliability. Spiritual perception follows *faith*. God doesn't measure the result but the faith itself. We saw the importance of faith above in Hebrews 4:2. God encourages us in Hebrews 5:14 to practice our spiritual perception with the trial and error that accompanies all learning:

> *Solid food is for the mature, who by constant use have trained their senses to discern good from evil.*

Your exercise of spiritual perception must be increasingly accurate to fulfill Hebrews 5:14, but not to meet some need or insufficiency God has. I Samuel 15:22 makes very plain what He wants.

> *Does the LORD delight in burnt offerings and sacrifices as much as in obeying the voice of the LORD? To obey is better than sacrifice, and to heed is better than the fat of rams.*

God wants you to heed His voice and obey it. By faith you trust that the accuracy of your perception is a responsibility He accepts, since giving you the perception was His idea in the first place. He is your Father, and you are safe with Him for the practice He wants. Do you expect your child to be perfect on every attempt?

This is not to discount the value of accurate spiritual perception. Earlier in I Samuel 2:35, it defined your priesthood—

> *I will raise up for Myself a faithful priest who will do according to what is on my heart and mind..*

We believers are those faithful priests, and I Peter 2:5 & 9 pick up on that theme. God regards our faithfulness as a commitment to the process of growing as a priest. As a result, all our desirable qualities increase, including accuracy in our spiritual perception.

15. **The enemies of God oppose your growth in spiritual perception with their last breath**. *"The god of this world has blinded the minds of unbelievers."* (II Corinthians 4:4) Satan relies on his ability to blind people. The apostles of the New Testament were acutely aware of the blinding that people suffered, preventing them from following the truth. Jesus identified as His mission the reversal of this blinding, in Luke 4:19.

When God has begun removing the blindfold on your perception, the enemies cannot restore their blindfold unless you cooperate with them. So next they attempt to confuse your perception. Paul tells of one strategy to confuse in II Corinthians 11:13-14—

For such men are false apostles, deceitful workmen, masquerading as apostles of Christ. And no wonder, for Satan himself masquerades as an angel of light.

He responds to another in Galatians 1:7-9—

Evidently some people are throwing you into confusion and are trying to pervert the gospel of Christ. But even if we or an angel from heaven should preach a gospel other than the one we preached to you, let him be eternally condemned! As we have already said, so now I say again: If anybody is preaching to you a gospel other than what you accepted, let him be eternally condemned!

John gives us an acid test in I John 4:1-3:

Do not believe every spirit, but test the spirits to see whether they are from God, because many false prophets have gone out into the world. This is how you can recognize the Spirit of God: every spirit that acknowledges that Jesus Christ has come in the flesh is from God, but every spirit that does not acknowledge Jesus is not from God. That is the spirit of the antichrist.

Spiritual perception results in awareness of our enemies & this is beneficial as Paul says in II Corinthians 2:11, *in order that Satan might not outwit us. For we are not unaware of his schemes.*

16. **Resisting God produces an inability to have spiritual perceptions**. In John 3, Nicodemus preferred reason and natural logic to justify believing Jesus. In verse 12, Jesus called attention to Nicodemus' resistance to spiritual perception, a resistance that was disabling the Jewish leaders' ability to believe.

I have spoken to you of earthly things and you do not believe; how then will you believe if I speak of heavenly things?

To the best Bible students of His day, Jesus spoke piercingly in John 5:38-47 about their lack of spiritual perception. By refusing Him and resisting Him, they lost their ability to understand the Scripture of Moses which they prized so highly.

You have never heard His voice or seen His form, nor does His word dwell in you, for you do not believe the one He sent. You diligently study the Scriptures because you think that by them you possess eternal life. These are the Scriptures that testify about me, yet you refuse to come to me to have life. I do not accept praise from men, but I know you. I know that you do not have the love of God in your hearts. I have come in my Father's name, and you do not accept me; but if someone else comes in his own name, you will accept him. But do not think I will accuse you before the Father. Your accuser is Moses, on whom your hopes are set. If you believed Moses, you would

believe me, for he wrote about me. But since you do not believe
what he wrote, how are you going to believe what I say?"

Later, religious listeners disqualified Him from speaking about
His own origins without a witness. This pattern of resisting him
caused Jesus to describe their spiritually dull perception in John
8:14,43.

You have no idea where I came from or where I am going....
Why is my language not clear to you? Because you are unable
to hear what I say.

Paul wrote likewise about these religious people. He knew them
and their resistance to God quite well, having been one of their
number:

Their minds were made dull (II Corinthians 3:14)

None of the rulers of this age understood it, for if they had, they
would not have crucified the Lord of glory (I Corinthians 2:8)

They are zealous for God, but their zeal is not based on
knowledge (Romans 10:2)

Moses understood well, in Deuteronomy. 29.4, that God's
judgment upon people for disobedience prevented their spiritual
perception:

The LORD has not given you a mind that understands or eyes
that see or ears that hear.

17. **You are accountable to use your spiritual perception
of what God shows you.** In modern language we might say, "use

it or lose it." You must take seriously your report on Judgment Day. God is revealing a new accountability to follow Him. He expects you to grow in the spiritual perception needed for the tasks He has for us.

Jesus told the parable of the talents in Matthew 25:14-30 to show that God will ask you what you did with the capacities He gave you. The talents were money in the parable, but the passage doesn't justify limiting His judgment to our material possessions. Jesus told the parable to describe His exercise of accountability in the Kingdom of Heaven. If you don't exercise your spiritual perception, a capacity He gave you for accomplishing His purposes, there is an accountability. You will incur the displeasure of Him who earned it for you and expects a return from you.

If you insist, you can keep your blindfold in place. People who believe Christian facts can refuse to grow their capacity for spiritual perception. They can be willfully blind. Jesus says of them in John 15:6,

If anyone does not remain in me, he is like a branch that is thrown away and withers; such branches are picked up, thrown into the fire and burned.

This mirrors the fate of the servant with the buried money who didn't fulfill the master's purpose and is thrown out as a worthless servant.

18. **Following Jesus *requires* you to activate your spiritual perception of His voice and leadership**. In John 20:21, Jesus sent us as His Father sent Him. Therefore the pattern for us following Him is the way He followed His Father, such as in John 5:19-21--

I tell you the truth, the Son can do nothing by Himself; He can only do what He sees His Father doing, because whatever the

*Father does the Son also does. For the Father loves the Son and
shows Him all He does. Yes, to your amazement, He will show
Him even greater things than these.*

This is a pattern of following what we spiritually perceive Him
to be doing and saying, just as He said about the faithful priest in I
Samuel 2:35. Jesus repeats in John 10:3-5 that this is the pattern for
you and me:

*The sheep listen to His voice. He calls out His own sheep by
name and leads them out. When He has brought out all His
own, He goes on ahead of them, and His sheep follow Him
because they know His voice... they will run away from a
stranger, because they do not recognize a stranger's voice. My
sheep listen to My voice; I know them and they follow Me.*

With this understanding of our pattern with Him being His
pattern with the Father, it is much clearer what Jesus meant when
He said in John 14:20 and 15:4,

*On that day you will realize that I am in my Father, and you
are in me, and I am in you.*
   Remain in me and I will remain in you.

Activating your spiritual perception is required for this. Without
spiritual perception, none of the above can occur at all.
   19. **Spiritual perception includes how you see yourself**.
In Jeremiah 1:10, the young Jeremiah protests his calling from God
based on how he sees himself.

*"Ah, Sovereign Lord," I said, "I do not know how to speak; I am
only a child."*

The Lord corrects him with a new self-perception, a decidedly spiritual one that has its origin in what God says Jeremiah is, and no other source. So in 1:7-10 Jeremiah gets a new self-image.

> But the LORD said to me, "Do not say, 'I am only a child.' You must go to everyone I send you to and say whatever I command you. Do not be afraid of them, for I am with you and will rescue you," declares the LORD.
> Then the LORD reached out his hand and touched my mouth and said to me, "Now, I have put my words in your mouth. See, today I appoint you over nations and kingdoms to uproot and tear down, to destroy and overthrow, to build and to plant."

To this could be added the example of Moses in Exodus 3-4. Jesus' own instruction in Matthew 7:1-3 presumes that spiritual perception includes yourself and even begins with yourself.

> Why do you look at the speck of sawdust in your brother's eye and pay no attention to the plank in your own eye? How can you say to your brother, 'Let me take the speck out of your eye,' when all the time there is a plank in your own eye?

It will not surprise you that this book will assist your spiritual self-perception to be more biblical. We grow up with ungodly beliefs about ourselves—"false identity statements." These are terms coined by Chester & Betsy Kylstra, founders of the highly effective Christian healing ministry, *Restoring the Foundations* (www.restoringyourlife.org).

Growing in spiritual perception will result in the gradual replacement of your false identity statements. True ones based on God's statements about you will govern your self-perception. Blindfold, be gone!

From the foregoing review of Scripture about spiritual perception, isn't it clear to you now that a Christian is a spiritually perceptive being? I hope that you want to receive this and activate your spiritual perception.

ACTIVATION 2-2

Read aloud the following statements, and after doing so, find two or three people and read the statements aloud to them. You can also record them, burn to a CD, and play them back in the car—which has helped me a lot over the years. We'll use the blanks later so just disregard them for now.

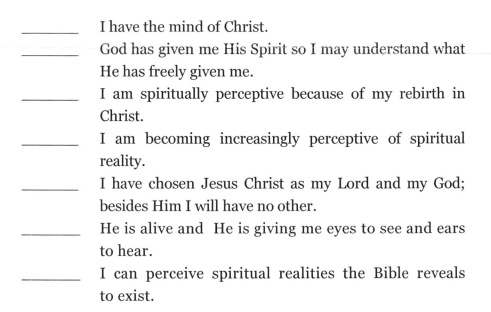

_____   I have the mind of Christ.

_____   God has given me His Spirit so I may understand what He has freely given me.

_____   I am spiritually perceptive because of my rebirth in Christ.

_____   I am becoming increasingly perceptive of spiritual reality.

_____   I have chosen Jesus Christ as my Lord and my God; besides Him I will have no other.

_____   He is alive and He is giving me eyes to see and ears to hear.

_____   I can perceive spiritual realities the Bible reveals to exist.

ACTIVATION 2-3

What is the present condition of your spiritual perception? Our last activation for this chapter is to establish a benchmark for your present spiritual perceptiveness. Answer as honestly as possible, without defensiveness, because you are accepted by God if you are a follower of Jesus. You will refer back to this later in the book. Mark your answers to the following statements on a scale of 1 being not true at all, or "I don't get it," to 5 being very true of you.

_____ When I speak, I am sometimes aware that the words are coming from God, or are not my own.

_____ I sometimes awaken with an awareness of God communicating with me or communing with me.

_____ I am sometimes aware of God showing me what to do in specific situations.

_____ Sometimes I feel compelled to say something specific to someone, or to pray something specific, & I wonder if it is God.

_____ I don't hear from God & wonder if I am saved, or if I am missing something.

_____ Sometimes pictures in my mind's eye capture my attention—and take priority over what my natural senses would normally perceive.

_____ I sometimes see qualities in my physical surroundings which are hard to express or understand but make me pause from normal activity.

_____ There are times I am aware of God's presence in or with me.

_____ There are times I feel compelled to speak or act with authority that doesn't seem normal for me.

_____ I wonder if people are aware of something about me which I haven't seen, because it seems they often act unexplainably toward me, either bad or good.

_____ I feel different from others and sometimes wonder if God supports me.

_____ I don't feel forgiven for some sin or another.

Now you have a benchmark of your present spiritual perception. Soon you can look back at them to realize how much you are growing, and how much perception of Scripture God is releasing to you now. I feel like a kid in a candy store, seeing what He is uncovering from Scripture for us.

The statements above come from the Scriptures themselves. You can verify this in Isaiah 50:4-9, Psalms 25 & 139, and I Corinthians chapters 12-14. The subsequent chapters will touch on these facts about you.

(P.S. If you also repeat aloud the above statements as if they are true, they will become evident in you more rapidly.)

Thank you, Father!
Thank you for leading me to remove my blindfolds!
I welcome Your light and sight into my eyes!

CHAPTER 3:
YOU ARE GOD'S BELOVED CHILD, HIS NAMED BENEFICIARY THOUGH COMPLETELY UNDESERVING, AND OBJECT OF HIS FAVOR

Have you ever been the beneficiary who received a life insurance benefit? Usually it is provided for you by someone you know and love, someone you depend upon, and they know and love you. But what if you learned you were the beneficiary on life insurance of Michael Jackson? The Pope? The President?

Your first thought would be, "why me?" Your second might be, "There must be some mistake." Then you might dare to think it actually is coming and you are going to have a huge sudden windfall. I say 'dare' because you might resist those thoughts so your hopes don't get up. After all, it just seems too good to be true. Face it, there is no reason this famous person should name you as beneficiary, or even know your name!

But this is how it is as a Christian.

I John 3:1 conveys the happy shock you can feel at this news!

How great is the love that the Father has lavished on us, that we should be called children of God! And that is what we are!

Paul exhibits the same overflowing exhilaration in a 237-word sentence in Ephesians 1, which includes 1:3 and 8.

Praise be to the God and Father of our Lord Jesus Christ, who has blessed us in the heavenly realms with every spiritual blessing in Christ! In accordance with the riches of God's grace that He lavished on us!

Let's imagine what it would be like, to learn that you were the beneficiary on the life insurance of a person whose son you had killed. They would definitely know your name! But where you expect hatred and retaliation or retribution, you learn that you are the named beneficiary on their life insurance--??!

Charles Wesley expressed the proper amazement and even incredulity in one of his greatest hymns:

> *And can it be, that I should gain*
> > *An interest in the Savior's blood?*
> *Died He for me, who caused His pain?*
> > *For me, who Him to death pursued?!*
> *Amazing love! How can it be*
> > *That Thou, my God, shouldst die for me?!*
> *Amazing love! How can it be*
> > *That Thou, my God, shouldst die for me?!*

But this is how it is for you, as a Christian.

Did you in fact cause His pain? Did you pursue him to death? Yes. You helped kill Jesus. In Acts 2:23, 37 & 3:14-15, the apostles hammered their listeners on this.

> *You, with the help of wicked men, put Him to death by nailing Him to the cross. ... God has made this Jesus, whom you crucified, both Lord and Christ. ... You handed Him over to be killed... you disowned the Holy and Righteous One... you killed the Author of Life. ...*

And their listeners got the message loud and clear: *You are determined to make us guilty of this man's blood!* (Acts 5:28) So, in 5:30, Peter made sure it was unmistakably clear:

> *The God of our fathers raised Jesus from the dead—whom you had killed by hanging Him on a tree.*

Perhaps nowhere is your undeserving nature as God's beloved former enemy clearer than Romans 5:8-10.

But God demonstrates His own love for us in this: while we were still sinners, Christ died for us. Since we have been justified by His blood, how much more shall we be saved from God's wrath through Him! For if, while we were God's enemies, we were reconciled to Him through the death of His Son, how much more, having been reconciled, shall we be saved through His life!

What are you, Christian? You are the beloved child of Someone from whom you have no right to expect anything. You are the beneficiary of all the benefits from the death of Someone you helped kill.

It's funny with God: the less you do to deserve this status of His beloved beneficiary, the more secure you are in it. After all, if this status was based on your just desserts, well, you could deserve to lose it also. But no—your selection as His beloved beneficiary was solely His choice. Though He had no reason to name you, He just did, out of pure love.

That's why Jesus designated as blessed the person He described in the Beatitudes of Matthew 5:1-12. Try reading it as a person with absolutely nothing you can contribute to your salvation. Each one is an attitude that results from this awareness. Each Beatitude after the other rises in your heart, one too poor to contribute anything at all.

Blessed are the poor in spirit,
for theirs is the kingdom of heaven.
Blessed are those who mourn,
for they will be comforted.
Blessed are the meek,
for they will inherit the earth.

Blessed are those who hunger and thirst for righteousness,
   for they will be filled.
Blessed are the merciful,
   for they will be shown mercy.
Blessed are the pure in heart,
   for they will see God.
Blessed are the peacemakers,
   for they will be called sons of God.
Blessed are those who are persecuted because of
righteousness,
   for theirs is the kingdom of heaven.

"Blessed are you when people insult you, persecute you and falsely say all kinds of evil against you because of me. Rejoice and be glad, because great is your reward in heaven, for in the same way they persecuted the prophets who were before you.

As your unblinded spiritual perception grows, it isn't your powers as a spiritual being that you see. Your spiritual perception pays attention to God above all else, and next to Him your spiritual poverty shines like an unhidable blemish. You perceive the gravity of your offense against Him. You perceive the high cost He has paid for it. You behold the downstream effect of your poverty of spirit on those He would have blessed, had you not been a poor sinner.

You gain a palpable awareness of your actual just desserts—damnation. You know deep within yourself that what the Father rightfully seeks—worshipers in spirit and in truth—is something only He can make you.

And that is blessed, Jesus says. This is totally backwards. How can this be?

He tells us why such a person is blessed. As you behold your spiritual poverty, your inheritance share as a prince or princess in the Kingdom of God is manifested. As you mourn your spiritual poverty and its cost to all that God intended, God Himself comforts you. This awareness of your thorough spiritual inadequacy makes you expect little, as one deserving no good, yet receiving from His hand the very earth itself.

You hunger and thirst for a manifestation on earth of the righteousness that you spiritually perceive. God satisfies you with the faith to enjoy it before it appears. You are merciful to others, bearing no pretense of superiority in yourself, and God pours endless mercy continually upon you.

In contrast, the leaders considered by the people to be rich in spirit were condemned and warned of damnation by Jesus, in Matthew 23 and John 8.

That's why Paul describes us in Ephesians 2:6-7 as the means by which God demonstrates His love to all the heavenly beings—we're the showpieces of His love. His love is powerfully on display when the poor in spirit are its recipients. The pride of God's enemies is humiliated by His choice of us.

And God raised us up with Christ and seated us with Him in the heavenly realms in Christ Jesus, in order that in the coming ages He might show the incomparable riches of His grace, expressed to us in His kindness to us in Christ Jesus.

Nor was this exclusively a New Testament revelation. Isaiah spoke God's word to us in 57:15 to the same effect, that you live with God and He lives with you, and that none of it is because you deserve it.

For this is what the high and lofty One says—He who lives forever, whose Name is holy--"I live in a high and holy place, but also with him who is contrite and lowly in spirit, to revive the spirit of the lowly and to revive the heart of the contrite."

Now so far in our book, we've reviewed what satisfies Jesus in His followers, and we yielded to the Scripture for understanding of our spiritual perception. But these are not how you come to deserve being God's beneficiary. No. You were God's beloved beneficiary before these things.

You see, a Christian is not someone who chooses God. Whatever environment your conversion occurred in, whether sudden or slow, it was God who chose you, and He chose you to be part of His many-membered Church.

This all occurred before He even made the world, plus, the Father made a present of you to Jesus! Consider the following.

> *All that the Father gives to Me will come to Me, and whoever comes to Me I will never drive away. For I have come down from heaven not to do My will but to do the will of Him who sent Me. And this is the will of Him who sent me, that I shall lose none of all that He has given Me, but raise them up at the last day... That is why I told you, that no one can come to Me unless the Father has enabled him.* (John 6:37-38, 65)

Two times Jesus speaks of you and all His followers as gifts from His Father. Now just how is it that we, with all our failings and shortcomings, are a gift to Jesus? You might feel insulted if someone gave you such a gift. Well, in Isaiah 49:1-7 and 53:11-12, God reveals why you and the Church are the gift that honors Jesus— the more saving He can do, the more He is honored and glorified, in the Father's opinion.

> *And now the LORD says..."It is too small a thing for you to be My servant to restore the tribes of Jacob and bring back those of Israel I have kept. I will also make you a light to the Gentiles, that you may bring My salvation to the ends of the earth....Therefore I will give [My servant] a portion among the great, and he will divide the spoils with the strong, because He poured out His life unto death, and was numbered with*

the transgressors. For He bore the sin of many, and made intercession for the transgressors.

Many Christians have trouble believing God could love them so much. They are confused by the enemies' attempts to confuse us and weaken our power. There are two particular enemy strategies to expose here. They trick us into adopting ungodly beliefs.

The first ungodly belief is, if something is too good to be true, it probably is. That is a lie. We use it day-to-day to sort out various advertising offers. But it contains a poison pill belief that sickens your faith: everything that is true must have some bad in it or have some string attached. This ungodly belief causes suspicion that God cannot be trusted to deal straight with you but in a sneaky way, with a "gotcha!" on the other end. Is this not the tone of satan's original temptation to Eve in Genesis 3:2-3?

Clearly, of all people, an undeserving beloved of God can and should believe that something too good can be true. ☐Agree ☐Disagree

The second ungodly belief is evident in the feeling that God's saving you depends at least a little on you. If it didn't depend on you, that would be too good to be true—right? But as covered in the last chapter—you are not measured by your accuracy or your love-worthiness. The Apostle John is plain about this in I John 4:10.

This is love: not that we loved God, but that He loved us and send His Son as an atoning sacrifice for our sins.

While we have a responsibility to be Jesus' followers, it is a responsibility that we can only fulfill because He unleashed a force of salvation within us and made His Holy Spirit to live in us. Titus 3:4-8 says,

But when the kindness and love of God our Savior appeared, he saved us, not because of righteous things we had done, but because of His mercy. He saved us through the washing of rebirth and renewal by the Holy Spirit, whom He poured out on us generously through Jesus Christ our Savior, so that, having been justified by His grace, we might become heirs having the hope of eternal life. This is a trustworthy saying. And I want you to stress these things, so that those who have trusted in God may be careful to devote themselves to doing what is good.

You, Christian, are an heir, chosen by God to be part of His Church before anything existed—and of course before you could contribute anything to the effort!

So here's your activations to help get this security into your heart as God's beloved.

ACTIVATION 3-1

First, stand up. Now shout as loud as you can--"I am God's beloved!"

ACTIVATION 3-2

Second, put yourself in God's shoes and write a letter to someone who is following Him, someone you know, other than yourself. Write based on this truth—that the person you are writing is a beloved of the Father, chosen though undeserving, and His beneficiary.

Thank you for removing this blindfold, Father!
I accept my status as Your beloved, and I cherish it.

CHAPTER 4:
YOU ARE ONE OF A NEW RACE OF MEN

Let's begin with an activation. To activate presumes that something is in you, but not active, rather awaiting your call to activate.

ACTIVATION 4-1

Please check an answer for each item below. All answers are okay and serve only for your own reflection and benchmarking.

YES MAYBE NO

☐ ☐ ☐ Sometimes I don't understand myself, not to mention others.

☐ ☐ ☐ I notice that sometimes I think really different from most people.

☐ ☐ ☐ It's hard to explain how I know what I know, even to myself.

☐ ☐ ☐ I wonder if people consider me weird.

☐ ☐ ☐ Sin attracts me less than ever.

☐ ☐ ☐ When I remember what I used to do and who I used to be, it seems like a different person, not me.

☐ ☐ ☐ It's harder than ever for me to indulge hostility or disregard for other people and other ethnicities.

☐ ☐ ☐ I enjoy Christian fellowship with surprising people I never thought I would enjoy.

☐   ☐   ☐   Heaven is on my mind a lot.

☐   ☐   ☐   Others evidence a feeling that I am not like them.

☐   ☐   ☐   When I look back on my sufferings I see so much good that I'm glad they happened.

☐   ☐   ☐   I often feel I am meant for something great even though my circumstances don't suggest this to be the case.

☐   ☐   ☐   It's easier to leave old behaviors, thoughts and feelings, which seem more and more useless as I drop them.

This was a benchmarking activation so you can see your own thoughts and have something to compare to as you read this chapter. I'm sure you have numerous yes's and maybe's.

What are you, Christian? You are one of a new race of men.

All the qualities and experiences you just read are from Scriptures which teach this truth. Without understanding the mystery God has revealed to us about His new Church race, you could easily feel weird, strange, alien, inferior and apologetic.

But with understanding of our new race, you are positioned for spiritual rulership and influence that dominates evil.

Apostle Peter addresses his first letter *to God's elect, strangers in the world.* He instructs his readers to *live your lives as strangers here* and calls them *aliens and strangers in the world.* (1:1,17, 2:11). This should show you that if you checked Yes or Maybe by the ones that reflect this truth, then you are on the right path. You are experiencing what the Bible says Christians should experience.

Apostle Peter isn't saying anything in this matter that he had not already heard straight from Jesus. At the Last Supper, Jesus surprisingly gives them a lot of teaching for the very first time, including this:

> *If you belonged to the world, it would love you as its own. As it is, you do not belong to the world, but I have chosen you out of the world. (John 15:16)*

He says the same thing twice to the Father as He prays:

> *They are not of the world any more than I am of the world....
> They are not of the world even as I am not of it. (John 17:14,16)*

Is Jesus saying this about you? Yes, if He considers you His follower. And it explains some if not all of your Yes's and Maybe's.

Notice the tone in what he says, and the context of it. In no way are Jesus or Peter implying that we are an inferior kind of strange, but rather, a superior kind of strange. Jesus emphatically puts you and the people who love Him in the same class as He is. This makes even more sense of I John 4:4, *He who is in you is greater than he that is in the world.* Far from being apologetic, we are meant to rule.

On what basis do Jesus and the New Testament writers say that you and I are strangers? We started with Apostle Peter and he identifies this cause:

> *[Our Father] has given us new birth....You have been born again, not of perishable seed but of imperishable, through the living and enduring word of God. (I Peter 1:3,23)*

And in this also Apostle Peter is echoing Jesus. Consider what Jesus said about you in John 3:3-8--

> *I tell you the truth, no one can see the kingdom of God unless he is born again. I tell you the truth, no one can enter the kingdom of God unless he is born of water and the Spirit. Flesh gives*

*birth to flesh, but the Spirit gives birth to spirit. You should
not be surprised at my saying, 'You must be born again.' The
wind blows wherever it pleases. You hear its sound, but you
cannot tell where it comes from or where it is going. So it is
with everyone born of the Spirit.*

Our culture has had exposure to (and media caricature of) being
born again. But the meaning of being born again has been held at
arms' length.

You and I are new beings. "Born" results in a new being. "Again"
signifies something different in kind from what was before. Jesus
says the something different is the Holy Spirit—we are the ones
who are spiritually alive. Notice above who the wind represents. It
does not represent the Holy Spirit. Rather, Jesus plainly says it is
everyone born of the Spirit. That means you are as unexplainable
and untraceable to the world as the wind.

And spiritually alive *like Him* we are—in John 8:14 He states
virtually the same thing about Himself that He says about you and
me.

As expected, Paul says the same thing in his classic statement of
our identity, Romans 6 through 8. The thread that makes sense of
these chapters is Paul's understanding of Jesus' followers as those
born of the Spirit. He writes of this as no mere add-on to a basic
Christian life; instead, Paul describes our spiritually alive existence
as the core of what a follower of Jesus is.

*We died to sin; how can we live in it any longer?...anyone who
has died has been freed from sin. ...the gift of God is eternal life
in Christ Jesus our Lord.* (6:2,7,23)

*by dying to what once bound us, we have been released from
the law so that we serve in the new way of the Spirit, and not
in the old way of the written code.* (7:6)

in order that the righteous requirements of the law might be fully met in us, who do not live according to the sinful nature but according to the Spirit. Those who live according to the sinful nature have their minds set on what that nature desires; but those who live in accordance with the Spirit have their minds set on what the Spirit desires. ...You, however, are controlled not by the sinful nature but by the Spirit, if the Spirit of God lives in you. And if anyone does not have the Spirit of Christ, he does not belong to Christ. But if Christ is in you, your body is dead because of sin, yet your spirit is alive because of righteousness. And if the Spirit of him who raised Jesus from the dead is living in you, he who raised Christ from the dead will also give life to your mortal bodies through his Spirit, who lives in you. ...those who are led by the Spirit of God are sons of God. For you did not receive a spirit that makes you a slave again to fear, but you received the Spirit of sonship. And by him we cry, "Abba, Father." The Spirit himself testifies with our spirit that we are God's children. (8:4-5, 8-15)

So far we have focused on you, the new being, as an individual. But that is not all there is to your new being. You are a member of *an entire race* of new beings, and it is in our plurality that our new being is completed. A large group of people so unique in one shared quality are called a race. The white race, the black race, the Asian race, the Arab race, to name just a few, are examples.

You are of the Spirit-born race. You are one of millions who are born not only of the flesh but of the Spirit.

Over the last few decades, the baptism of the Holy Spirit has been viewed as the hallmark of the charismatic and Pentecostal segments of the Church. Christians have differed in understanding Scripture about receiving and growing in the Holy Spirit, and uniformity is not required to benefit from this workbook. What is at stake for each lover of Jesus is not what denomination you are—it is whether you are a member of the Spirit-born race. After all, the lover of Jesus seeks all of Him, no holds barred. ❑Agree ❑Disagree

Expressions of our Spirit-born race vary among Christians, for He is indeed described in Revelation 4 as "the seven-fold Spirit," that is, too big and too complete for us to define. There is no biblical expectation that all Jesus' followers will worship the same or act the same or conform to the same code of non-moral behaviors. Variety is welcomed in His kingdom.

However, some variety exists only because Christians say to God, "this far, and no farther." Some variety exists only because Christians seek to use God rather than follow Him. These and other types of willfully immature discipleship reveal that Christians limit the Holy Spirit's influence in their lives. Perish the thought of limiting God's Lordship. The judgment and accountability on the worthless servant who didn't satisfy his master's wishes is an experience every Christian must be vigilant to avoid.

Therefore consider these Scriptures on our racial identity as people born brand new, as spiritually alive beings. Through the prophet Joel, in 2:28-29, God described the new man that He would create:

> *And afterward,*
> *I will pour out my Spirit on all people.*
> *Your sons and daughters will prophesy,*
> *your old men will dream dreams,*
> *your young men will see visions.*
> *Even on my servants, both men and women,*
> *I will pour out my Spirit in those days.*

We saw that after the Resurrection, Jesus opened his disciples' minds to understand the Scriptures (Luke 24:45) and spoke to them about the kingdom of God (Acts 1:4). Peter's sermon on Pentecost suggests that this Joel passage was among those that Peter and the apostles studied in the upper room. Peter spoke therefore of the rebirth in and filling of the Spirit as the key promise itself—a surprising new common identity.

Then Peter stood up with the Eleven, raised his voice and addressed the crowd: "Fellow Jews and all of you who live in Jerusalem, let me explain this to you; listen carefully to what I say. These men are not drunk, as you suppose. It's only nine in the morning! No, this is what was spoken by the prophet Joel:

In the last days, God says,
  I will pour out my Spirit on all people.
Your sons and daughters will prophesy,
  your young men will see visions,
  your old men will dream dreams.
Even on my servants, both men and women,
  I will pour out my Spirit in those days,
  and they will prophesy....

Exalted to the right hand of God, he has received from the Father the promised Holy Spirit and has poured out what you now see and hear. ...Repent and be baptized, every one of you, in the name of Jesus Christ for the forgiveness of your sins. And you will receive the gift of the Holy Spirit. The promise is for you and your children and for all who are far off —for all whom the Lord our God will call." (Acts 2:17-19, 33,38-39)

What is Peter's invitation? We now use the words, "to be saved." Are you surprised to see that Peter speaks of repenting, baptism and the forgiveness of sins as steps to, but not as, the final desired result? Instead, like Jesus and John the Baptist before Him, Peter lays these out as the necessary steps to receiving the promised Holy Spirit. Is this not what Jesus said in John 3:6-8 above?

Nor was Joel the only prophet through whom God revealed His plan to make a new race of people, unique because of His Spirit alive in them. Ezekiel received the same revelation from God in 36:26,37 & 37:14.

I will give you a new heart and put a new spirit in you; I will remove from you your heart of stone and give you a heart of flesh. And I will put my Spirit in you and move you to follow my decrees and be careful to keep my laws. ...I will put my Spirit in you and you will live, and I will settle you in your own land.

Paul's letters to the Corinthian church are well-known for addressing many church problems—but less well known is his basis for rebuking them:

Brothers, I could not address you as spiritual but as worldly —mere infants in Christ. I gave you milk, not solid food, for you were not yet ready for it. Indeed, you are still not ready. You are still worldly. For since there is jealousy and quarreling among you, are you not worldly? Are you not acting like mere men? For when one says, "I follow Paul," and another, "I follow Apollos," are you not mere men? .... Don't you know that you yourselves are God's temple and that God's Spirit lives in you? (I Corinthians 3:1-4,16)

Therefore, if anyone is in Christ, he is a new creation; the old has gone, the new has come! (II Corinthians 5:17)

Paul's comments to the Corinthians tell us that we are no longer "mere men" and therefore should not act like one.

We are of one race with Jesus because we are reborn in His image—as spirits made alive. Jesus' very purpose as revealed to John the Baptist was not forgiveness of sins. Forgiveness of sins was prelude, characterizing John's repentance ministry. John spoke clearly of Jesus' purpose in Luke 3:16—*He will baptize you with the Holy Spirit and with fire.* Forgiveness of sin might be as far as *we* want to go, but to Jesus and the apostles, it was just the beginning, a necessary step to our true calling: rebirth as newly formed Spirit-dominant persons like Jesus.

Forgiveness of sins is certainly both necessary and one of our greatest blessings from God. But when a Christian says to God, "that's all I want; no farther," that's dangerous disagreement with God. With our sin forgiven, God can live in us as His temple—even if we don't perceive it, like the Corinthians. He sent Jesus to enable this through forgiveness of sin—the birth of a new, Spirit-born, Spirit-dominant race, in the image of Jesus.

Apostle John also writes of us being in Jesus' image in I John 3:2--

Dear friends, now we are children of God, and what we will be has not yet been made known. But we know that when he appears, we shall be like him, for we shall see him as he is.

Paul understood our racial identity with Jesus as central to God's purpose for us in the other half of a familiar verse, Romans 8:28-29. We are called according to His purpose for us which is what?

And we know that in all things God works for the good of those who love him, who have been called according to his purpose. For those God foreknew he also predestined to be conformed to the likeness of his Son, that he might be the firstborn among many brothers.

This is no mere behavioral conformity but a core identity of being like Him in our nature. It is that identity we share with Jesus that makes us one race. This identity clearly trumps all other commonalities, race and gender both, as Paul says in Galatians 3:26-29 with clearly racial language.

> *You are all sons of God through faith in Christ Jesus, for all of you who were baptized into Christ have clothed yourselves with Christ. There is neither Jew nor Greek, slave nor free, male nor female, for you are all one in Christ Jesus. If you belong to Christ, then you are Abraham's seed, and heirs according to the promise.*

You may be white and I may be white, but if I love Jesus and you don't, I am more like Him than I am like you. You may be black and I may be white, but we both love Jesus, we are more like each other than you are like blacks and I am like whites.

Jesus taught the disciples at the Last Supper, in John 17:16, that we are not of the world. No classification the world uses is adequate to distinguish us.

> *They are not of the world, even as I am not of it.*

That tells you what you are *not*. Through Apostle Paul, in Colossians 2:9 & 3:1-4, God revealed what you *are—*

> *For in Christ all the fullness of the Deity lives in bodily form, and you have been given fullness in Christ, who is the head over every power and authority. ...Since, then, you have been raised with Christ, set your hearts on things above, where Christ is seated at the right hand of God. Set your minds on things above, not on earthly things. For you died, and your life is now hidden with Christ in God. When Christ, who is your life, appears, then you also will appear with him in glory.*
>
> *Both the one who makes men holy and those who are made holy are of the same family. So Jesus is not ashamed to call them brothers. (Hebrews 2:11)*

The next two passages drive home that you are not a solitary Spirit-born person, but a member of a new race, the Church race. In Ephesians 2 Paul uses the plural "you" to describe us as "one new man:"

> As for you, you were dead in your transgressions and sins, ...we were by nature objects of wrath. ...But because of his great love for us, God, who is rich in mercy, made us alive with Christ even when we were dead in transgressions ...At that time you were separate from Christ, excluded from citizenship in Israel and foreigners to the covenants of the promise, without hope and without God in the world. ...For he himself is our peace, who has made the two one and has destroyed the barrier, the dividing wall of hostility, by abolishing in his flesh the law with its commandments and regulations. His purpose was to create in himself one new man out of the two, thus making peace. (Ephesians 2:1, 3-4, 12-15)

The New Testament teaches us that we cannot be a Spirit-born person without being in a Spirit-born race, as in I Peter 2:9-10--

> you are a chosen people, a royal priesthood, a holy nation, a people belonging to God, that you may declare the praises of him who called you out of darkness into his wonderful light. Once you were not a people, but now you are the people of God; once you had not received mercy, but now you have received mercy.

In numerous ways the NT writers applied our racial identity to our group behavior. One such is I John 2:19 where John tells us how we know someone is not of our race as the Spirit-born:

They went out from us, but they did not really belong to us. For if they had belonged to us, they would have remained with us; but their going showed that none of them belonged to us.

The New Testament repetition of our identity as one new racial family gives new activation to a commonly known command. Jesus commanded us to love one another. Without the old blindfold, you see loving one another is not merely a behavior of niceness, nor even works of service only. It is our core identity as people of one Spirit. It is a shared racial uniqueness, which Jesus and the NT writers considered the core of who we are. This is why we are not of the world—because we are born of the flesh and of the Spirit, unlike them. And so Jesus states: *By this will all men know that you are my disciples, if you love one another.* (John 13:35)

ACTIVATION 4-2

Let's revisit your benchmarking activation at the first of this chapter—here reworded. This time, simply check the statements which you feel you can accept, based on the Scriptures we have considered.

- ❒ When I don't understand myself, it might be my spiritual nature seeking my recognition.
- ❒ When I feel different from others, I will rejoice that Jesus chose me out of the world.
- ❒ When I know something but don't know how I do, I'll ask the Holy Spirit if it is from Him.
- ❒ When I feel weird in society, I will yield to God's belief that His people are the superior stranger here, not the inferior ones.
- ❒ I expect that maturing in Jesus' image will cause all kind of sin to lose power over me.
- ❒ When I seem like a different person compared to my past, I will rejoice in being Spirit-born!

☐ I delight in the variety of people that God has called to love Jesus and welcome them as the same race as me.

☐ My attraction to heaven is an expression of my spiritually alive being, a signal of my eternity.

☐ When others express I am unlike them, I testify about being born of the Spirit and urge them to enjoy it for themselves.

☐ Hardship results in more of Jesus in me, and in more of His life for His spiritual nature in me.

☐ I yield to what the Spirit says about my great destiny, more than I yield to my circumstances.

☐ As my living spirit matures, behaviors and attitudes I once permitted myself are easy to drop.

ACTIVATION 4-3

For your final activation, to help you perceive continually your membership in this new race as a new being and stranger of superior standing to the world, pick 4 of the statements above and write them on post-it notes or index cards that can remind you of your new racial identity.

That's biblical too—Deuteronomy 6:7-8.

Holy Spirit, I accept my identity as a new man born of You in Your new race of men. Thank you for removing my blindness to this.

CHAPTER 5:
YOU ARE A SPIRIT-DOMINANT CREATURE, SUSTAINED THROUGH YOUR SPIRIT

So far in our book, we've seen who Jesus considered to be His followers. We saw in Matthew 7:20-21 that miracles, prophecy and driving out demons do not make someone a follower of Jesus.

We've reviewed lots of Scripture teaching about your spiritual perception. We have identified you as an undeserving beloved of Almighty Holy God. Your new being as a Holy Spirit-born person makes you one of a new race of men.

One by one, blindfolds are being removed from your spirit's perception and you are waking up to what you are. As a child, did you ever enjoy looking under rocks to see what was there? This chapter is about the heaviest rock you will have to lift, and the most enjoyable treasures lie waiting under it for you and your friends to see.

Think about what lies behind you. Maybe you used to think Jesus would be satisfied if someone simply verbalized the sinner's prayer and held certain beliefs. You used to dismiss the perceptions of your spirit. You used to think that God wouldn't love you unconditionally unless you met some standard, a standard often used to accuse you and induce inferiority in your self-assessment.

And you used to think of yourself simply as a person with Jesus-centered beliefs and behaviors, not as a newly formed being, part of a newly formed race.

Did the first chapters fit with things you have been experiencing? Everything we've covered, all the transformations and privileges of being God's child, became available to you the day you first followed

Jesus. But this chapter may be hard for you and we will spend more time on this truth.

Blindfolds make our eyes used to the dark. When it is removed and you open your eyes, the light is so bright that you shut them back immediately. It takes time for your eyes to adjust. Same here—you are giving your outlook the opportunity to adjust to the beautiful light you have just begun to see.

You may even want to spend a few days digesting this chapter since so much of your life's thought-environment and viewpoint has been contrary to what you are about to read in the Bible.

Let's start with food. Clearly our Father will feed us the physical food we need, Jesus said in Matthew 6:25-32.

> *Therefore I tell you, do not worry about your life, what you will eat or drink; or about your body, what you will wear. Is not life more important than food, and the body more important than clothes? Look at the birds of the air; they do not sow or reap or store away in barns, and yet your heavenly Father feeds them. ... So do not worry, saying, 'What shall we eat?' or 'What shall we drink?' or 'What shall we wear?' For the pagans run after all these things, and your heavenly Father knows that you need them.*

ACTIVATION 5-1

☐Yes ☐No Will you yield to His promise to feed, clothe and shelter you as reliable?

☐Yes ☐No Will you trust His Fatherhood more than you trust what you see in circumstances?

☐Yes ☐No Will you rebel like Satan thinking you can do better than God can for you?

☐Yes ☐No Will you believe Satan's accusation that God is an unreliable Father?

YES, YES, NO, NO are what we aim for in those four questions. Now let's expand our view of what Fatherly promises God makes about our food and our relationship with physical creation as Spirit-dominant new beings.

Jesus led the woman at the well to faith in him. Afterward, his disciples brought him food and in John 4:31-34, Jesus shows you how we live in our new race.

> *Meanwhile his disciples urged him, "Rabbi, eat something." But he said to them, "I have food to eat that you know nothing about." Then his disciples said to each other, "Could someone have brought him food?" "My food," said Jesus, "is to do the will of him who sent me and to finish his work."*

In saying that, as in many things He said, Jesus is demonstrating living by a promise of God, a promise through a prophet. In Isaiah 55:1-3, God describes life as His beloved.

> *Come, all you who are thirsty, come to the waters; and you who have no money, come, buy and eat! Come, buy wine and milk without money and without cost. Why spend money on what is not bread, and your labor on what does not satisfy? Listen, listen to me, and eat what is good, and your soul will delight in the richest of fare. Give ear and come to me; hear me, that your soul may live.*

Jesus was a man of the Scriptures. He also learned from Moses, and relied on what God said through Moses about physical food, in Deuteronomy 8:3.

> *Man does not live on bread alone but on every word that comes from the mouth of the LORD.*

Repeatedly God identifies one kind of food as dominant for His people, and another kind as secondary. Unquestionably, spiritual food must dominate your life.

ACTIVATION 5-2

For your first activation let's consult your memory. Before going further in this chapter, to prepare you for the full benefit of what follows, please write a few words about a time or incident when eating food became a secondary concern—even to the point of others reminding you or begging you to eat something.

_____

_____

_____

_____

You are not alone. Every Spirit-born person has this window on their spiritual nature, a sign that there is more to you than what physical food nourishes. There is a you that needs a higher nourishment. Food became secondary in that event because something else became a more primary expression of yourself, a more primary source of sustenance.

Jesus experienced this also, in Mark 3:20-21.

> *Then Jesus entered a house, and again a crowd gathered, so that he and his disciples were not even able to eat. When his family heard about this, they went to take charge of him, for they said, "He is out of his mind."*

This is the same Spirit-dominant living He expressed to His disciples in John 4:32-34 above. He also showed it when there was severe threat to His physical well-being, in Mark 4:37-38—

> *A furious squall came up, and the waves broke over the boat, so that it was nearly swamped. Jesus was in the stern, sleeping on a cushion. The disciples woke him and said to him, "Teacher, don't you care if we drown?"*

His ability to sleep in that environment demonstrates life as a Spirit-born person—and how He and we are definitely not of this world as seen in the previous chapter. That peaceful assurance during sleep is also our birthright as His followers. Anxieties that awaken you are attempts to keep you from enjoying a sleep founded on your dominant identity—a spirit made alive as God's child.

After feeding the 5,000 recorded by Apostle John in John 6, Jesus speaks very plainly again about the secondary place of physical food. We Christians are so blessed—check this out from verses 24-27. As the crowd saw it, they had just identified their source of free food.

Once the crowd realized that neither Jesus nor his disciples were there, they got into the boats and went to Capernaum in search of Jesus. When they found him on the other side of the lake, they asked him, "Rabbi, when did you get here?"

Jesus answered, "I tell you the truth, you are looking for me, not because you saw miraculous signs but because you ate the loaves and had your fill. Do not work for food that spoils, but for food that endures to eternal life, which the Son of Man will give you."

Jesus wants them to see the multiplication of the loaves and fishes as a miraculous sign. A sign of what? That a more primary food than physical food is at hand in limitless abundance—a food that is given, and that endures to eternal life. Once again we see Him teaching what God had said in the Old Testament. And Jesus plainly wants you and me and all His followers, to understand what food must receive our primary longing—the food that Spirit-born people require.

For a person in our materialistic society which trains us to easily rationalize our priority upon the observable world, it may be hard to understand or accept this. I suggest you read those verses again, doublecheck the interpretation offered, and decide if you will obey it. You are commanded to prioritize your spiritual food over your physical food, so circle one:

❒ YES ❒ NO I will work primarily for food which Jesus gives me, that endures to eternal life.

Jesus further defines that food in 6:33,35, & 51-58—

> *it is my Father who gives you the true bread from heaven. For the bread of God is he who comes down from heaven and gives life to the world....Then Jesus declared, "I am the bread of life. He who comes to me will never go hungry, and he who believes in me will never be thirsty. ...I am the living bread that came down from heaven. If anyone eats of this bread, he will live forever. This bread is my flesh, which I will give for the life of the world. ...I tell you the truth, unless you eat the flesh of the Son of Man and drink his blood, you have no life in you. Whoever eats my flesh and drinks my blood has eternal life, and I will raise him up at the last day. For my flesh is real food and my blood is real drink. Whoever eats my flesh and drinks my blood remains in me, and I in him. Just as the living Father sent me and I live because of the Father, so the one who feeds on me will live because of me. This is the bread that came down from heaven.*

Maybe like Jesus' pursuers that day, you have found these statements by Jesus to be bizarre and puzzling: *On hearing it, many of his disciples said, "This is a hard teaching. Who can accept it?"* (6:60) They all left—5,000 plus. They had just eaten free food and thought they had it made because they saw physical food as dominant. They were unwilling for this error to be corrected by Lord Jesus.

The key to receiving Jesus' puzzling remarks is to identify and understand yourself predominantly as a person born of the Spirit, and to live primarily as a Spirit-born person. Jesus says this Himself when the event nears its conclusion in John 6:62-63. All but twelve of his disciples left him because of what you just read.

> *Jesus said to them, "Does this offend you? What if you see the Son of Man ascend to where he was before! The Spirit gives life; the flesh counts for nothing. The words I have spoken to you are spirit and they are life."*

Peter speaks for the twelve when he affirms, *"Lord, to whom shall we go? You have the words of eternal life."* (6:68)

The dominance of your spiritual needs over your physical needs is throughout Scripture and well-practiced throughout church history. It is only temporarily forgotten in our modern materialistic world system. Mankind is fundamentally religious, seeking always to regain spiritual life in one way or another. Our materialistic way of seeing the world is opposed to thinking and living as a Spirit-born person. Without even knowing it is an issue, you are in agreement with materialism. You've signed onto that way of seeing. You have agreed to wear a blindfold. You're not alone, of course—so have the majority of Western Christians. That's one reason Western churches and Christians have until recently manifested so little real power over the observable world.

ACTIVATION 5-3

Here's another window on your spirit, and on your agreement with this materialistic world system. Do you indulge every desire of your body? ☐Yes ☐No

Most of us are chuckling and checking No. Keep going.

Do you indulge every emotion you have? ☐Yes ☐No

Do you indulge every thought you have? ☐Yes ☐No

Have you done things or sought experiences which you expected satisfaction from but which gave you little if any? ☐Yes ☐No

God has given His people a life-detector—your spirit. It was reborn when you yielded your life to Jesus. Your spirit is where your best, most enduring satisfaction is enjoyed. Your soul and your body can certainly have enjoyable experiences and effective actions. But they do not bring the life of the Spirit. In fact, the satisfaction of soul and body can kill the life of your spirit. That's why Apostle Paul writes in Galatians 5:17, 25 and Romans 8:5-6.

For the sinful nature desires what is contrary to the Spirit, and the Spirit what is contrary to the sinful nature. They are in conflict with each other, so that you do not do what you want.... Since we live by the Spirit, let us keep in step with the Spirit.

*   Those who live according to the sinful nature have their minds set on what that nature desires; but those who live in accordance with the Spirit have their minds set on what the Spirit desires. The mind of sinful man is death, but the mind controlled by the Spirit is life and peace....*

Your spirit within is mighty to dominate your body and your soul. Your soul includes your mind, emotions and beliefs about how the world works. It's easy to see that if you always do what your body wants, you'll become a mess quickly. The same is true with your soul—but it's harder to see. If you always do what your soul dictates, you also become a mess, a never-satisfied soulish person.

But satisfy your spirit, and soul and body quickly follow suit. Is your soul craving peace? Then feed your spirit before the Lord God, and your soul will be quieted. David described doing this in Psalm 131:2-3.

But I have stilled and quieted my soul;
   like a weaned child with its mother,
   like a weaned child is my soul within me.

O Israel, put your hope in the LORD
  both now and forevermore.

In our history as a Church, men of their times sought to dominate their bodies through self-inflicted pain. Without placing judgment on them, we can now say confidently that the Scripture doesn't justify this. Instead, God has made us so that satisfying our spirit takes care of the other needs and elevates our spirit to pre-eminence in our life.

Paul describes living as a Spirit-dominant person several times in I Corinthians. For instance, about how his ministry related to his eating in 9:14-15:

> *If we have sown spiritual seed among you, is it too much if we reap a material harvest from you? If others have this right of support from you, shouldn't we have it all the more? But we did not use this right. On the contrary, we put up with anything rather than hinder the gospel of Christ....I have not used any of these rights. And I am not writing this in the hope that you will do such things for me. I would rather die...*

This is the speech of someone whose attention is on the food that doesn't spoil, that endures to eternal life. And did you notice what he says he will put up with?

ACTIVATION 5-4

☐Yes ☐No I am willing to put up with anything rather than hinder the gospel of Christ.

☐Yes ☐No ANYTHING.

☐Yes ☐No I will give up eating before I hinder the gospel!

☐Yes ☐No I've got to come back to this before I can check Yes to all those.

ACTIVATION 5-5

Paul lists in I Corinthians some ways that he demonstrates living as spirit-dominant over his physical being. In the blank, pick a name for the area of life where Paul's comment shows spirit-dominant living. Names such as business, travel, family, eating, social relationships.

_____ *Though I am free and belong to no man, I make myself a slave to everyone, to win as many as possible.* (9:19)

_____ *I beat my body and make it my slave so that after I have preached to others, I myself will not be disqualified for the prize.* (9:27)

_____ *Why do we endanger ourselves every hour? I die every day —I mean that, brothers.* (15:30)

_____ *When I came to you, brothers, I did not come with eloquence or superior wisdom as I proclaimed to you the testimony about God. For I resolved to know nothing while I was with you except Jesus Christ and him crucified. I came to you in weakness and fear, and with much trembling. My message and my preaching were not with wise and persuasive words, but with a demonstration of the Spirit's power, so that your faith might not rest on men's wisdom, but on God's power.* (2:1-5)

_____ *"Everything is permissible for me"—but not everything is beneficial. "Everything is permissible for me"—but I will not be mastered by anything. "Food for the stomach and the stomach for food"—but God will destroy them both.* (6:12-13)

Paul tells the Corinthians the truth that enables him to live this way in I Corinthians 6:19-20.

The body is not meant for sexual immorality, but for the Lord, and the Lord for the body. ...Do you not know that your body is a temple of the Holy Spirit, who is in you, whom you have received from God? You are not your own; you were bought at a price. Therefore honor God with your body.

No wonder Paul could tell the Philippians in 4:12,

I have learned to be content whatever the circumstances. I know what it is to be in need, and I know what it is to have plenty. I have learned the secret of being content in any and every situation, whether well fed or hungry, whether living in plenty or in want. I can do everything through him who gives me strength.

Paul did not live primarily as a physical being nor did he prioritize his physical needs higher than his spirit-born living. He did not let his soul dictate how he lived, either. His living spirit, like yours a spirit in communion with God Almighty, was the boss of his soul and body.

ACTIVATION 5-6

☐Yes ☐No My body is meant for the Lord, and the Lord is meant for my body.

☐Yes ☐No The Holy Spirit is in me and my body is His place on this earth.

☐Yes ☐No My lips are Jesus' lips now and He gets primary say-so in what's done with them.

☐Yes ☐No My senses are Jesus' senses now and He gets primary benefit in my use of them.

☐Yes ☐No I will not be mastered by my physical body or by the material world, but only by My Master.

We started with nourishment, sustenance and food as one key area that our Spirit-born nature can dominate. What about miracles? That's something every Christian strongly desires. How do we, as

Spirit-dominant newly formed beings, relate to the physical creation now?

Let's define miracles. Using Webster's online dictionary, a miracle is an extraordinary event manifesting divine intervention in human affairs. Certainly after all we've read so far, we now question the use of the word "intervention." That word suggests interruption, un-natural, and suspension of the normal. And people celebrate miracles because miracles are unexpected and rare (if ever) for them—not normal at all.

Well, our norm is being Spirit-born, and our normal is living as Father's undeserving beloveds, a new race of new spiritually alive beings He has formed. And we do not regard miracles as the rare, unexpected thing. We celebrate miracles but not as beggars hoping for crumbs, or warriors too blind and timid to take what is theirs. Miracles prove that our normal is breaking in. Miracles demonstrate in this world the fuller, most-true world where we live and function— the world of spirits made alive.

ACTIVATION 5-7

Jesus sets our expectations repeatedly and plainly. See for yourself—did Jesus consider miracles rare for you, or as normal? Check your answers after reading the passage.

❑Rare ❑Normal   *"Have faith in God," Jesus answered. "I tell you the truth, if anyone says to this mountain, 'Go, throw yourself into the sea,' and does not doubt in his heart but believes that what he says will happen, it will be done for him. Therefore I tell you, whatever you ask for in prayer, believe that you have received it, and it will be yours."* (Mark 11:21-22)

❑Rare ❑Normal   *These signs will accompany those who believe: In my name they will drive out demons; they will speak in new tongues; they will pick up snakes with their hands; and when they drink deadly poison, it will not hurt them at all; they will place their hands on sick people, and they will get well.* (Mark 16:17-19)

❏Rare ❏Normal *The seventy-two returned with joy and said, "Lord, even the demons submit to us in your name." He replied, "I saw Satan fall like lightning from heaven. I have given you authority to trample on snakes and scorpions and to overcome all the power of the enemy; nothing will harm you."* (Luke 10:18-19)

❏Rare ❏Normal *I tell you the truth, anyone who has faith in me will do what I have been doing. He will do even greater things than these, because I am going to the Father. And I will do whatever you ask in my name, so that the Son may bring glory to the Father. You may ask me for anything in my name, and I will do it.* (John 14:12-13)

❏Rare ❏Normal *If you remain in me and my words remain in you, ask whatever you wish, and it will be given you. This is to my Father's glory, that you bear much fruit, showing yourselves to be my disciples.* (John 15:7)

❏Rare ❏Normal *In that day you will no longer ask me anything. I tell you the truth, my Father will give you whatever you ask in my name. Until now you have not asked for anything in my name. Ask and you will receive, and your joy will be complete. Though I have been speaking figuratively, a time is coming when I will no longer use this kind of language but will tell you plainly about my Father. In that day you will ask in my name. I am not saying that I will ask the Father on your behalf. No, the Father himself loves you because you have loved me and have believed that I came from God.* (John 16:25-27)

Clearly Jesus considers miracles to be the norm for someone following Him. Do you think He would regard it as an arbitrary divine intervention? Not at all. If you are a Spirit-born, Spirit-dominant person, "miracles" are the expected result of someone walking with God, living as a functioning spirit, and representing God's favor upon men. Such a person might define miracles as acts of Spirit-dominant rulership by God and His people. And what could be more normal than that for us?

This can be hard for us in Western civilization. It's harder for you to understand life as foundationally spiritual than it is for people of non-Western cultures. But you must grow to that point. What you just read is Jesus telling you what you are, Christian, and what He intends to be done by people such as you.

You can rationalize keeping the blindfold that makes the natural world seem primary. You can neglect your truest identity as a spirit-dominant person. But this is rebellion, isn't it? An argument with God? If God says in His Word that you have this identity, you do.

It is a hard thing I write but as you saw in John 6, He himself weeded out those who would not go with Him in this matter. He fed them, meeting their physical needs so they would come into the Spirit-dominant life. But when they said, "this far and no further," He showed them the door in John 6:63-66.

The words I have spoken to you are spirit and they are life. Yet there are some of you who do not believe." For Jesus had known from the beginning which of them did not believe and who would betray him. He went on to say, "This is why I told you that no one can come to me unless the Father has enabled him."

From this time many of his disciples turned back and no longer followed him.

❏Yes ❏No Is that what you want for your outcome?

Notice—the disciples turned away from words that are spirit and life. Your fleshly nature is always moving away from them. This is why your living spirit must dominate your body and soul. The Holy Spirit quickly endorses every determination you make to do so.

These disciples who would not go all the way with Jesus are like the worthless servant we discussed earlier. He rationalized his failure. He would not attempt the master's expected return on investment. He was banished, just as these disciples were.

In fact, when you rationalize your own failure to live as a Spirit-born person, what God desires for this earth through you is in jeopardy. The consequences are astounding. Unless you and I mature into Spirit-sensitive people, we may miss the need of people He brings before us. Without practiced perception, you may not notice the person whose spiritual birth is delegated to your midwifery. If you bow to the enemy taunt of "not being spiritual all the time," you may be led astray unawares.

Add up all the consequences and it's no wonder the Church has required 2,000 years to mature into what we now are. It is the sum of centuries—our willful blindness to living as people born of God's Spirit.

I do not want to be willfully blind anymore. ❏Yes ❏No Are you with me?

Jesus said His follower must give up everything and we limit the word "everything" to mean our physical stuff. Of course that's how materialistic people would understand him—physical stuff is most important to them. But "everything" includes our right to dictate how we see the world. It includes our expectation of fitting in with the world. "Everything" reaches into your mind and the very way you see yourself.

You cannot be what you are, Christian, if you are unwilling to perceive what Jesus sees.

He sees you as a living, functioning spirit. Your identity as a spirit-dominant creature explains why speech, words, names, and other communication actions are so prominent in the Bible. Words are how spirit is expressed in this natural world. That's why Peter said what he did to Jesus: *You alone have the words of life.*

Whatever natural there is, God spoke into being. And now you have seen your identity as a living spirit. He spoke that identity. The natural cannot choose against God's spoken Word, but you? He lets you keep your blindfolded identity as a natural-dominant being if you choose—but it's a tragedy.

This is where the rubber meets the road for us Western Christians. Funny, isn't it? We find it easy to believe the virgin birth, easy to accept that God became man, easy to believe that Jesus' death actually had some impact on our sins because we simply believe, and most shocking of all, easy to accept the idea that God loves us. But it's a lot harder for us to believe that Almighty God could heal someone, supply our finances, feed us, and work with us on practical material things. If you can relate to this, then you now see your materialistic viewpoint. As a materialist, it is easy to believe Christian truths that don't have much to do with your actual day-to-day material world, and it is very hard to believe God for the far, far lesser challenges that are practical and day-to-day in nature.

Why is this? Really, it's backwards and embarrassing that we so easily believe the super challenging truths, but we resist believing the easy realities that naturally follow those truths.

We must admit that the force of sin is active in us and rebels against everything God. When God says "you are xyz," sin in me immediately contradicts and says, "I can't be xyz, I'm not xyz, I'll never be xyz." Sin's voice may be more subtle too, less blatant but an argument with what God says nonetheless. "One day I'll be xyz." "I'm xyz if I can act xyz."

Sin also rebels by drawing lines. Yes, we'll have maybe A and B about God, but we draw the line at C and D. Church, okay; reliance upon His forgiveness, okay—but let His presence in me be the determining factor of my agenda today? Let Him dominate my thoughts? "That's where I draw the line" is the answer seen in how we live the day.

For this sin in you and in me we must actively and repeatedly repent. Sure you're forgiven but the offense is new every morning. Active repenting is the surest way to be blessed as Jesus made plain in the Beatitudes. The penitent is the one who is poor in spirit, mourning, meek and hungry. And the absence of repenting is the surest sign of willful blindness and sin's refusal to yield to what God says is the way things really are.

The sin in you works with a powerful blindfold mentioned above—a systemic sin in Western civilization called materialism. It comes from a philosophy called naturalism. You spent 12+ years in school with this view of the world assumed, like the water a fish swims in. Our Western education for 100 years has been committed to the lie that the physical is primary, and the spiritual only exists secondarily, to fill gaps left by the physical among other things. That is the world-view that sees miracles as "divine intervention."

This worldview also elevates the soul above the spirit. Either way—your body dictating your life, or your soul dictating—the enemy scheme of materialism successfully silences and obscures your powerful spirit. That spirit functionality is what our enemies fear most. You are in Jesus' image. What could possibly be more threatening to God's enemies than a large number of activated Jesuses on the earth? That's one reason there's so much enemy investment into building up blindfolds and kneading them as systemic sin into the world's view.

This soul elevation is evident in the popular understanding of psychology—a term compounded from the Greek words for soul and organizing principles. Professional psychologists and established counseling methods are effective and not to be disdained. But in the popular conception of it, a poison pill belief has gained acceptance: that your soul runs the show. And it most emphatically doesn't have to—for you, that is.

Instead, as a living spirit, you are shedding the blindfold of that systemic sin. Our enemies develop systemic sin because the force of Jesus' resurrection life in us is too great for only our sin nature to resist by itself, unassisted.

You are and have been every day of your Christian life an undeserving beloved of a Holy God, a spiritually perceptive newly formed member of the new race of men, and a Spirit-born person.

The only thing different is that now you are coming to perceive this to be true of you.

As a result, you can now perceive the most normal, the most real world—the spiritual world in which you live as a Spirit-dominant person. You can now correct the erroneous residue in your head of the physical-dominant education you received. You can now receive everything God installs into every day as the main thing going on—not just your soul and body stuff, but your vital spirit-feeding communion with Him.

This most real world is what the 24 elders on the thrones in heaven see every single moment that exists, according to Revelation 4:11. Note both the past and the present tenses in God's creating:

> *You are worthy, our Lord and God,*
>   *to receive glory and honor and power,*
> *for you created all things,*
>   *and by your will they were created*
>   *and have their being.*

You are free from the prison of the physical-dominant perspective. You no longer have to listen to the sin in you. This sin wants you to live as if your well-being is more threatened by what you see in the physical than by disobeying your loving Father.

Now you see why many Christians and churches have little if any practical spiritual power in this world. We have prayed for miracles to occur which did not. We have inspected our faith to see if it was "enough." We have attended conferences to keep our faith at miracle-working level. Yet little changes, and decay infiltrates our society further at every level. How can this be, with so many Christians?

Christians and churches have created many explanations for this failure to meet Jesus' expectations for every believer. One is that miracles ceased when the first generation apostles died. Another is that God only intervenes in societies where mankind hasn't developed a solution. And sadly, many have abandoned hope of miracles, buried under the mocking laughter of their materialistic presuppositions.

Be easy on yourself if this is you. God has been bringing you on a journey. He has you in a process. Everything builds to the present and He will work in you to manifest the perfection He has decreed for you. So don't fault yourself for your previous unawareness. Just repent and keep going. Repeat that daily. Be blessed in the process, like those whom Psalm 84:5 describes:

Blessed are those whose strength is in You, who have set their hearts on pilgrimage.

Remember, early on, Jesus flatly said to the disciples, *you know nothing about* it (John 4:34). But later, He brought things to their awareness and said, *from now on you do know* (John 14:7).

☐Yes ☐No Can you trust Him to manage your awareness?

Apostle Paul describes this awareness management in Romans 12:1-3. God's part is to transform your mind. The church that is bereft of power limits this to doctrine and other more intellectual things. Yes, those are included for sure. But the transformation occurs on the basis of our surrender of our bodies, our physical-dominant view. Self-denial is our part. And the result is our fuller recognition of God's will. There is no more guessing game about what God's will is.

Therefore, I urge you, brothers, in view of God's mercy, to offer your bodies as living sacrifices, holy and pleasing to God—this is your spiritual act of worship. Do not conform any longer to the pattern of this world, but be transformed by the renewing of your mind. Then you will be able to test and approve what God's will is —his good, pleasing and perfect will.

Apostle Peter says in I Peter 4:1-2 that suffering in the flesh enables us to live for the will of God; we no longer live for evil human desires. He says this because paying the cost with our physical selves makes everything become clear. Suffering forces us to realize that our natural selves are not primary, but rather our spirits are. Suffering exposes our willful blindness.

In 4:2-5 of his letter, James gives us a great explanation of why we live willingly in unawareness, and he tells us what to repent of.

You do not have, because you do not ask God. When you ask, you do not receive, because you ask with wrong motives, that you may spend what you get on your pleasures. You adulterous people, don't you know that friendship with the world is hatred toward God? Anyone who chooses to be a friend of the world becomes an enemy of God. Or do you think Scripture says without reason that the spirit he caused to live in us envies intensely?

First he described those who abandoned hope of miracles and belief in the dominance of the Spirit over the physical. Then he zeroes in on our starting point when we do ask—as if the physical world dominates. He says our motive and our view of how things work are all like the 5,000 who pursued Jesus after receiving free food—we are in agreement or friendship with the world. So how can God gladly do as we ask, if our starting point in our minds is idolization of the physical world over the unseen spiritual world?

Quite the contrary—when we start there, it incites His jealousy over us and He shuts down what He otherwise loves to do and has promised to do. Even if we ask a good thing He likes doing, He must not answer us if our heart is in agreement with the world as to the pre-eminence of the physical. Answering our requests while we are in friendship with the world artificially spares us the corrective pain that such wrong-headedness should cause.

The right-headedness is to be like Paul says in II Corinthians 4:18.

So we fix our eyes not on what is seen, but on what is unseen.
For what is seen is temporary, but what is unseen is eternal.

We Spirit-born beings are accountable to God, to allow Him the full use of our full beings to establish His kingdom. To do this we must live as Spirit-dominant people, for that is what you are, Christian.

Apostle John gives us guidance in I John 5:14-15 for praying in friendship with God rather than friendship with the world.

This is the confidence we have in approaching God: that if we
ask anything according to his will, he hears us. And if we know
that he hears us—whatever we ask—we know that we have
what we asked of him.

A materialist sees in those statements a guessing game about what God wants in any given situation. That's because materialistic thinking considers the observable physical world as the primary reality. But John is emphasizing that spirit-dominant people make different requests than physical-dominant people. Put on your self-concept as one who is Spirit-born and Spirit-dominant, and then read John's next comments, in 5:18-20.

> We know that anyone born of God does not continue to sin; the one who was born of God keeps him safe, and the evil one cannot harm him. We know that we are children of God, and that the whole world is under the control of the evil one. We know also that the Son of God has come and has given us understanding, so that we may know him who is true. And we are in him who is true—even in his Son Jesus Christ.

That's you. That's what you are, Christian. Alright! Yea, Lord! With the same self-concept, let's re-visit what Jesus said to pray for in Matthew 6:9-13.

> Our Father in heaven, hallowed be your name, your kingdom come, your will be done on earth as it is in heaven. Give us today our daily bread. Forgive us our debts, as we also have forgiven our debtors. And lead us not into temptation, but deliver us from the evil one.

This prayer is far, far more practical if you are praying it as a Spirit-dominant person. You aren't someone just hanging on by a thread with God, begging for something good to occur. Instead, you pray as a member of His people, a newly formed race of men. You pray as His deputized and authorized beloved. You agree with Him what steps should be taken today.

That's a huge improvement over the way we used to pray, when God's actions were interventions from a distant unaffected heaven. No wonder people reacted to Jesus in Matthew 9:8,

> When the crowd saw this, they were filled with awe; and they praised God, who had given such authority to men.

Jesus controls the rate of your dawning awareness of what you are, Christian. He removes blindfolds in His timing. Now you will see Apostle Paul say something about you that has been true of you the entire time of your Christian life. There is only one difference between your unaware past and your spiritually perceptive future. You now can enjoy and be what you are, Christian—and Jesus now gets to enjoy His full capability in you. That's what He has been envisioning for you, as His home and temple on the earth. What a fulfilling future awaits!

I suggest you buckle yourself in and read the following as many times as it takes to believe it about yourself. It's in the Bible. It is clearly stated about every Christian. You are a Christian. It is true about you, so check one:

❑I will ❑I will not   believe what the Bible says about me.
❑I will ❑I will not   believe what the Bible says about all
                        Jesus' followers including me.

Here you go—I Corinthians 2:10-16 is written to Paul's most difficult, immature church, as if to say all followers of Jesus, mature and immature, are this.

The Spirit searches all things, even the deep things of God. For who among men knows the thoughts of a man except the man's spirit within him? In the same way no one knows the thoughts of God except the Spirit of God. We have not received the spirit of the world but the Spirit who is from God, that we may understand what God has freely given us. This is what we speak, not in words taught us by human wisdom but in words taught by the Spirit, expressing spiritual truths in spiritual words. The man without the Spirit does not accept the things that come from the Spirit of God, for they are foolishness to him, and he cannot understand them, because they are spiritually discerned. The spiritual man makes judgments about all things, but he himself is not subject to any man's judgment:

"For who has known the mind of the Lord that he may instruct him?" But we have the mind of Christ.

You have the mind of Christ. That's who you are.

For the entire duration of this chapter, I have been including little quickie activations for you. Let's end with more thoughtful ones. (But first, do you need to revisit Activation 5-4?)

ACTIVATION 5-8

Name a time when your prayer for a miraculous intervention was not answered. For me, it was when my mom died.

_____

_____

_____

Now sit silently for 3 minutes with this question in your heart for God: "At that time, was I asking as someone dominated by the physical?" A clue that you might have been: you considered it rare, an intervention, or a suspension of the physically dictated normal.

_____

_____

_____

Write down how you decided or assumed what to pray.

_____

_____

_____

Now name a time you felt a desire within to pray for some miracle but were afraid to ask.

_____

_____

_____

Why were you afraid to ask for that one?

_____

_____

_____

ACTIVATION 5-9

Name a time that a sign of the new normal has occurred (what you used to call a rare miracle) that you did not even ask for.

_____

_____

_____

_____

ACTIVATION 5-10

Now list 2 or 3 present problems or concerns you have right now, ones that require solutions nothing you see can solve.

1. _____
2. _____
3. _____

Now get a clock in view and let's see how the normal of a Spirit-born, Spirit-dominant person comes about. For each one of these, sit silently for 3 minutes. Wait on God. Don't talk with your voice or your mind. Just wait on Him with one questioning attitude and one readiness only in your heart: *What do You want me to pray, Father?* As you wait on Him, jot down what pictures you see in your mind's eye, what you sense and perceive, what thoughts come into your mind.

1. _____
2. _____
3. _____

Okay—pray what you just wrote. Don't judge it with your mind. Aren't you spiritually perceptive? Surely after waiting on your loving Father for direction on what to pray, you have enough confidence in Him to pray what He says pray? And isn't it His prerogative to tell you what to pray, as unusual as it might be? After all the Scripture is full of people led by Him into very unusual and strange encounters.

Just pray what He said to pray. Is that so hard?

"God, I think it is You telling me to pray these things. I really want to live as the Christian You say that I am. I repent for my willful blindness to what You have revealed in Scripture. Please uphold me in stepping out on this limb with You and Your Bible. So You said to pray X, and I am obeying you. Please remove my blindfolds."

If you need a Scriptural reference for this because it seems so weird—I Samuel 15:22-23 and John 12:49-50 are just two we could choose.

Does the LORD delight in burnt offerings and sacrifices
*   as much as in obeying the voice of the LORD?*
To obey is better than sacrifice,
*   and to heed is better than the fat of rams.*
For rebellion is like the sin of divination,
*   and arrogance like the evil of idolatry.*

For I did not speak of my own accord, but the Father who sent me commanded me what to say and how to say it. I know that his command leads to eternal life. So whatever I say is just what the Father has told me to say.

Father, I repent for being willfully blindfolded
to the identity You have spoken for me.
Thank you for opening my eyes!

CHAPTER 6:
YOU ARE A CREATURE IN CONTINUAL COMMUNION AND REST WITH YOUR CREATOR

Does this chapter's title alone challenge your credulity? How can a Christian be said to have continual communion and rest with God? Is it hard to believe?

That's why faith and belief will be subjects in this chapter also. Consider the fish. He swims in water that forms his complete and constant environment. Does he notice it? We assume he doesn't unless he is taken out of his water environment.

I don't know what fish "think" so let me use my own example. In 1990 I worked at a printer. I remember that the first day I walked in to apply, there was such a strong pungent odor of ink I felt nauseated. Within a day of working there, I no longer noticed it. Visitors would come and comment on the nauseating smell. It surprised me that what I had once considered a strong unbearable odor was no longer noticeable to me.

In the same way, there is water that your thinking is swimming in, a constant and total environment that you do not notice without effort. It may smell really bad without you even noticing it. So let's begin with a benchmark activation.

ACTIVATION 6-1

❏Yes ❏No I do have continual communion and rest with God.

❏Yes ❏No I am aware of having continual communion and rest with God.

❏Yes ❏No When I come to be alone with God, agitation often blocks me.

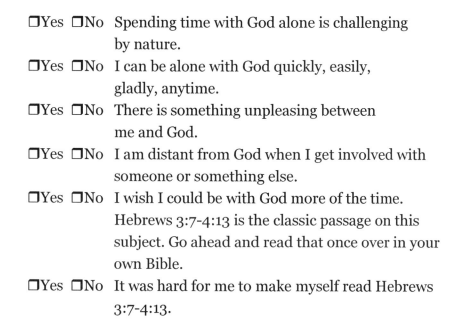

☐Yes ☐No Spending time with God alone is challenging by nature.

☐Yes ☐No I can be alone with God quickly, easily, gladly, anytime.

☐Yes ☐No There is something unpleasing between me and God.

☐Yes ☐No I am distant from God when I get involved with someone or something else.

☐Yes ☐No I wish I could be with God more of the time. Hebrews 3:7-4:13 is the classic passage on this subject. Go ahead and read that once over in your own Bible.

☐Yes ☐No It was hard for me to make myself read Hebrews 3:7-4:13.

In Hebrews 3:18-19, the Holy Spirit clearly connects rest, faith & obedience.

And to whom did God swear that they would never enter his rest if not to those who disobeyed? So we see that they were not able to enter, because of their unbelief.

You may have one of two responses to that Scripture. Each response reveals an inward self-assessment you live with, like the water the fish swims in. We'll look at each of the two responses in turn but let's begin with Hebrews 3:12-14.

See to it, brothers, that none of you has a sinful, unbelieving heart that turns away from the living God. But encourage one another daily, as long as it is called Today, so that none of you may be hardened by sin's deceitfulness. We have come to share in Christ if we hold firmly till the end the confidence we had at first.

Look at the sin that God pinpoints here. It is not violation of a behavior code. Instead, God pinpoints the attitudes and worldviews in us—overarching agreements by which we govern ourselves. This agrees with all that we have seen previously. Notice the one-two punch—a sinful unbelieving heart, and the hardening of sin's deceitfulness (our minds being full of deception originated by sin). The opposite of these conditions is to hold firmly our confidence—more on that later. We used a phrase earlier to signify these overarching agreements and ways of seeing things: ungodly beliefs.

So the first response people have, "I don't know of a disobedience or a disbelief in my life." You may be unable to pinpoint something that keeps you out of continual communion with God. Yet your communion with God is in fact changing and not continual. It feels episodic, occasional, or vanishing. You may feel close to Him during worship or some other such Christian action, but distant during other actions.

The second response is this. You are aware of or feel constantly ashamed about a disobedience or a disbelief. You may feel that you know exactly what keeps you from entering God's rest. You've confessed it and repented of it—yet it hangs over you. You keep hoping for freedom, seeking counsel. You may even be resigned to it for the rest of your life. It may torment you so that you wonder if you can make it another day. The devil condemns you, and you may even confuse it with God's voice.

Both responses reveal a way of thinking about your relationship with God that requires correction if this book accurately captures what God is saying.

ACTIVATION 6-2

☐25% ☐50% ☐75% ☐100%
is how accurate about Scripture I would say this book is so far.
☐25% ☐50% ☐75% ☐100%
is how accurate about me I would say this book is so far.

☐25% ☐50% ☐75% ☐100%

is how accurate the activation exercises have been so far.

The purpose for that activation was to give you and God a common basis for discussing the corrective truths that lies ahead in this chapter.

God has given us two excellent examples in Scripture of people with the two inward responses described above.

As for the first response, it's wonderful if you are aware of no disobedience or disbelief in your life. Truly this is to be desired and enjoyed. But why is it, then, that you aren't experiencing continual communion and rest with God? After all, according to Hebrews 3:18-19 if you are aware of no disobedience or disbelief you should be entering God's rest, right? If you are not entering God's rest, it may signify that you have an ungodly belief: that your relationship with God is code-based. Let's investigate that, so you can have a sign to recognize and to make corrections.

The Jewish leaders had that code-based self-assessment—they evaluated themselves based on code conformity. We see it in John 9:16,24,29 & 34, where they questioned the once-blind man whom Jesus had healed on the Sabbath.

> Some of the Pharisees said, "This man is not from God, for he does not keep the Sabbath."...A second time they summoned the man who had been blind. "Give glory to God," they said. "We know this man is a sinner. ...We are disciples of Moses! We know that God spoke to Moses, but as for this fellow, we don't even know where he comes from." ..."You were steeped in sin at birth; how dare you lecture us!" And they threw him out....

Jesus described this kind of Bible person in John 5:37-40, conforming to code but without life.

> You have never heard his [the Father's] voice nor seen his form, nor does his word dwell in you, for you do not believe the one

he sent. You diligently study the Scriptures because you think that by them you possess eternal life. These are the Scriptures that testify about me, yet you refuse to come to me to have life.

That's troubling, isn't it? Yet it is as possible to be a Bible student and not obey Jesus, as it is to do miracles, drive out demons and prophesy without Him knowing you (Matthew 7:20-21). We can think we are fine and yet be lost as a goose. This is why Hebrews warns us against *a sinful, unbelieving heart* and a mind *hardened by sin's deceitfulness.*

These warnings in Hebrews 3 highlight the problem of assessing yourself by some code of behavior or thought. You can be aware of no disobedience or unconformity, yet you are not having communion with God. If you aren't hearing Him in your spirit, the previous chapters may have seemed like something that you just couldn't grasp. If you have accepted that He has to be far away unless you are in a Christian activity, then don't look to some code to find out where you are going wrong. You don't lack faith, or knowledge, or teaching.

Why not? Because you don't have a belief problem and you don't need more teaching. My advice to you is to do what I do: get on your knees and humble yourself before God as often as you can.

Make that your first spiritual response, your fundamental attitude, and your attitude of heart—not self-measurement by a code of conformity. Sin will find no home in a lowly spirit or contrite heart.

Jesus said that *many are called but few are chosen.* (Matthew 22:14) It was religious people, Bible students, who killed Him. How can you hope to escape that blindness? You can't—and that's why He provides the simplest of actions for your escape: repenting quickly and often, casting your poor spirit upon Him. He says in Isaiah 57:15,

For this is what the high and lofty One says—
  he who lives forever, whose name is holy:
"I live in a high and holy place,

but also with him who is contrite and lowly in spirit,
to revive the spirit of the lowly
and to revive the heart of the contrite.

Alleluia! What relief!

From this it's clear that God blesses us by our repentance and poverty of spirit. He's not measuring us by performance or perfection. You don't have to inspect yourself for things you do or don't do, things approved or condemned. Instead vigilantly repent and cast yourself on Him.

You rest in your Father's love. Just get on top of the ladder and fall back and let Him catch you. These Scriptures plainly say that the follower of Christ has continual communion and rest with God, and for one reason: He lives in you, and no other reason, no contribution of your own.

The second self-assessment is exhibited by Job's three friends, Eliphaz, Bildad and Zophar. They are a tremendous resource for understanding an incorrect view of God and our relationship because God flatly says they spoke wrongly about Him and that Job spoke correctly about Him (Job 42:7).

These men also represent the viewpoint that our relationship with God is transactional. It might be described this way: *God is out there somewhere or everywhere. If I give Him what He wants, I will get what I want.*

For all his speech born of heartache, Job spoke accurately about God, that God isn't distant and disengaged, measuring one's life in a tit-for-tat of obedience and observance. Job didn't like what he felt God was doing to him, but he never gave up his insistence that God was personally engaged with him and knew him in a personal relationship, as we see in Job 13:15 and 19:25-27.

Though he slay me, yet will I hope in him;
I will surely defend my ways to his face. ...

I know that my Redeemer lives,
and that in the end he will stand upon the earth.
And after my skin has been destroyed,
yet in my flesh I will see God;
I myself will see him
with my own eyes —I, and not another.
How my heart yearns within me!

We've dwelt on these two self-assessments to pull off a blindfold, a prominent deceit that Christendom has fallen under—that our relationship with God is fundamentally transactional. Most Christians and churches are swimming in a water that believes this:

God is out there somewhere, or everywhere. If I give Him what
He wants, I will get what I want.

This is the origin of many Christians' frustration because there is no way to win at this. Consider your unanswered prayers in view of Hebrews 11:1.

Now faith is being sure of what we hope for and certain of
what we do not see.

How often have you wanted something from God, and made sure to believe that He would do it, so that He would do it? Really—does the "God" in that viewpoint sound like a God at all? Yet this is the impact of the transactional thinking about you and God. That is having faith in your faith and God works to get you off that dead-end road.

Notice how the transactional blindfold locks you into ignoring the obvious failure of that formula for the prophets who were killed, listed shortly afterward in Hebrews 11:35-38. They are listed as examples of those who had faith, who were certain of what they hoped for. The author of Hebrews actually uses their deaths and torture to illustrate their faith.

Having faith in our faith is not the way God relates to us, as much as we might try to force Him to. He refuses manipulation and shuts down the blessings we seek when we attempt it. On top of that, God simply is not predictable or controllable. (Neither are we. Recall John 3:8, that we who are born of the Spirit are as unpredictable and uncontrollable as the wind.)

The fact is, God flatly repudiates the transactional view of man's relationship with God. We saw earlier James' remarks about this, in James 4:2-5. Instead of motivating God, it incites His jealousy to be our first love. The church in Ephesus was reprimanded for this also in Revelation 2:2-4.

Hebrews shows God's repudiation of the transactional relationship with Him. Consider 8:3,5 & 6.

> *Every high priest is appointed to offer both gifts and sacrifices, and so it was necessary for this one also to have something to offer. ...They serve at a sanctuary that is a copy and shadow of what is in heaven. ...But the ministry Jesus has received is as superior to theirs as the covenant of which he is mediator is superior to the old one, and it is founded on better promises. For if there had been nothing wrong with that first covenant, no place would have been sought for another.*

Yet we who call ourselves Christians and Christian churches continue relating to God like people under the Old Covenant. Listen to our prayers, our hymns, our cries and our counsel. Listen in on our evangelism and our missions. Is there not a strong belief that God is usually out there, not with us constantly, and somehow we have to bring Him close if we want closeness with Him? Once you see it, you cannot *not* see it.

God, praise His name, replaced the transactional system of the Old Testament covenant with a new one. Hebrews goes on to describe it in 8:8-12 by quoting 31:31-34 of the prophet Jeremiah. As you read it, let yourself relax. It is what you are, Christian.

But God found fault with the people and said:

"The time is coming, declares the Lord,
  when I will make a new covenant
with the house of Israel
  and with the house of Judah.
It will not be like the covenant
  I made with their forefathers
when I took them by the hand
  to lead them out of Egypt,
because they did not remain faithful to my covenant,
  and I turned away from them,
declares the Lord.
This is the covenant I will make with the house of Israel
  after that time, declares the Lord.
I will put my laws in their minds
  and write them on their hearts.
I will be their God,
  and they will be my people.
No longer will a man teach his neighbor,
  or a man his brother, saying, 'Know the Lord,'
because they will all know me,
  from the least of them to the greatest.
For I will forgive their wickedness
  and will remember their sins no more. "

By calling this covenant "new," he has made the first one obsolete; and what is obsolete and aging will soon disappear.

Could it be any plainer than that last sentence, Hebrews 8:13?
God also reveals in Hebrews His replacement for the transactional relationship—something we might call a "confidence relationship."

And it is this confidence relationship that activates our continual communion and rest with our Creator.

This confidence relationship brings a rest to your spirit, that no matter what code you may violate, no matter how poverty-stricken your spirit is, no matter what battles you lose, no matter what spiritual leaders may say about you, no matter how naked you are before God, nothing can alter your communion and rest with God.

The only thing that varies is your awareness. In that area you can grow. But the reality itself, regardless of your awareness of it, never ever changes.

David wrote a sweet, otherwise puzzling expression of this in Psalm 139:18.

When I awake, I am still with you.

Doesn't it seem different? I think the transactional viewpoint would write it this way: "When I awake, You are still with me." The transaction mindset expects that God comes and goes based on whether we pay attention to Him or give Him what He wants. Of course we cannot do that while we sleep. But this Scripture tells you, it is only your awareness that fluctuates, in this case by sleeping. It is not God who comes and goes.

A confidence relationship results in a constant rest in God. That is fertile soil for a constant knowing God, and a continual pleasure in who He is, how He acts, and what He wants. Awareness flowers and grows in a confidence relationship. I know of no passage that describes it better than what God said through Isaiah in chapter 32. Below are selected verses to highlight what you really are, Christian—really and truly, in actual fact, in reality, regardless of your awareness of it. Regardless of the accuracy of your beliefs, the conformity of your behavior, or your acceptance by the leadership—so read and enjoy the new creation that God has made you into.

See, a king will reign in righteousness
    and rulers will rule with justice.
Each man will be like a shelter from the wind
    and a refuge from the storm,
like streams of water in the desert
    and the shadow of a great rock in a thirsty land.

Then the eyes of those who see will no longer be closed,
    and the ears of those who hear will listen.
The mind of the rash will know and understand,
    and the stammering tongue will be fluent and clear.
No longer will the fool be called noble
    nor the scoundrel be highly respected....

But the noble man makes noble plans,
    and by noble deeds he stands. ...

The fortress will be abandoned,
    the noisy city deserted;
citadel and watchtower will become a wasteland forever,
    the delight of donkeys, a pasture for flocks,
till the Spirit is poured upon us from on high,
    and the desert becomes a fertile field,
    and the fertile field seems like a forest.
Justice will dwell in the desert
    and righteousness live in the fertile field.
The fruit of righteousness will be peace;
    the effect of righteousness will be quietness and confidence
forever.
My people will live in peaceful dwelling places,
    in secure homes,
    in undisturbed places of rest.
Though hail flattens the forest
    and the city is leveled completely,
how blessed you will be,

sowing your seed by every stream,
and letting your cattle and donkeys range free.

Wow! That is what you are, Christian. Talk about entering rest. Rest even if the hail destroys everything. A confidence relationship is truly the abundant life Jesus spoke of.

So you don't experience that rest? That doesn't take away from the reality of it, for God has said that you have a confidence relationship with Him now and forever. Circumstances have no authority to dispute or discredit what God has said. That's the meaning of what Paul writes in Romans 3:4—*Let God be true, and every man a liar.* And we might add, every circumstance a liar, when it contradicts what He has said about you.

Hebrews describes the transactional relationship and its failings again, in 10:1-4.

The law is only a shadow of the good things that are coming—not the realities themselves. For this reason it can never, by the same sacrifices repeated endlessly year after year, make perfect those who draw near to worship. If it could, would they not have stopped being offered? For the worshipers would have been cleansed once for all, and would no longer have felt guilty for their sins. But those sacrifices are an annual reminder of sins, because it is impossible for the blood of bulls and goats to take away sins.

He doesn't use the word "transaction" but he is certainly describing your former self-assessment that your communion and rest in God is not continual.

So he goes on to tell us again about our confidence relationship in 10:9-10.

First he said, "Sacrifices and offerings, burnt offerings and sin offerings you did not desire, nor were you pleased with them" (although the law required them to be made). Then he said, "Here I am, I have come to do your will." He sets aside the first to establish the second. And by that will, we have been made holy through the sacrifice of the body of Jesus Christ once for all.

The "once for all" element terminates your need for constant self-assessment of where God is with you. "Once for all" means DONE. PERMANENT. As in "IT IS FINISHED."

God implements this confidence relationship in you by living in you directly. Hebrews 9:15 echoes the apostles' identification of the promise as the indwelling Spirit of God, and says,

For this reason Christ is the mediator of a new covenant, that those who are called may receive the promised eternal inheritance —now that he has died as a ransom to set them free from the sins committed under the first covenant.

To the New Testament apostles, this promised inheritance of the Holy Spirit, this assurance that God lives in you, was the death-knell of the transactional relationship with God. The transactional outlook says that God is out there & must be satisfied, and it has been called obsolete. Peter said in Acts 2:38-39,

Repent and be baptized, every one of you, in the name of Jesus Christ for the forgiveness of your sins. And you will receive the gift of the Holy Spirit. The promise is for you and your children and for all who are far off —for all whom the Lord our God will call.

Stephen was killed by the Jewish leadership, in Acts 7:51-53. Why? because he fingered the failures of the transactional relationship to its chief defenders—

"You stiff-necked people, with uncircumcised hearts and ears! You are just like your fathers: You always resist the Holy Spirit! Was there ever a prophet your fathers did not persecute? They even killed those who predicted the coming of the Righteous One. And now you have betrayed and murdered him —you who have received the law that was put into effect through angels but have not obeyed it."

God demonstrated powerfully that He had ended the transactional relationship using a vision before Peter's encounter with the Gentiles in Cornelius' home. The apostles regarded it so highly that Luke twice told it in Acts 10 and 11. God three times says to Peter, *Do not call unclean what God has made clean.* (Acts 10:15) Peter watches as the Holy Spirit falls on uncircumcised, unclean, unbaptized Gentiles—and Roman soldiers at that—even before they prayed the Sinner's prayer. What could he do, he later explained in 11:17, but instruct that these men be baptized into the name of the Lord Jesus?

There is some comfort to realize that the Jerusalem-based church had a similar problem to us—that the transactional relationship with God still lingered in their thinking. We know this because they heavily criticized Peter for baptizing such people. And God emphatically repudiated the transactional view again as they clearly recognized, even with shock and incredulity, after Peter's explanation in Acts 11:15-17—

As I began to speak, the Holy Spirit came on them as he had come on us at the beginning. Then I remembered what the Lord had said: 'John baptized with water, but you will be baptized with the Holy Spirit.' So if God gave them the same gift as he gave us, who believed in the Lord Jesus Christ, who was I to think that I could oppose God?"

When they heard this, they had no further objections and praised God, saying, "So then, God has granted even the Gentiles repentance unto life."

God the Spirit living in you is how you have continual communion and rest with God. It is the birthright of the Spirit-born.

Christian, where God is with you never changes—He is in you. That's why you are a new creation (II Corinthians 5:17). It's not because you behave better. It's because He came to live in you and you are a two-will being, one of a new race.

Your awareness changes. Your feelings change. Your obedience changes. The change is positive in general with fluctuations along the way. If you charted your changes, it might look like a yo-yo going up and down while the "yo-yo-er" walked up stairs. But a confidence relationship as taught in Hebrews is unchanging.

Your communion with God can only vary if He comes and goes. If you think that, then sin's deceitfulness has tricked you back into the transactional view of God's walk with you.

The only possible change to it is for us to abandon God, or for it never to be a confidence relationship in the first place. Consider Hebrews 6:4-6, 10:26-27, 35-36—stern alerts to take very seriously.

It is impossible for those who have once been enlightened, who have tasted the heavenly gift, who have shared in the Holy Spirit, who have tasted the goodness of the word of God and the powers of the coming age, if they fall away, to be brought back to repentance...Even though we speak like this, dear friends, we are confident of better things in your case—things that accompany salvation.

If we deliberately keep on sinning after we have received the knowledge of the truth, no sacrifice for sins is left, but only a fearful expectation of judgment and of raging fire that will consume the enemies of God....So do not throw away your confidence; it will be richly rewarded. You need to persevere so that when you have done the will of God, you will receive what he has promised.

Resolve that you will always be vigilant to live in your confidence relationship with God. *Do not throw away your confidence!*

The Galatians give us the best New Testament warning about Christians who abandon their confidence relationship and resume the transactional view. Paul tells them in Galatians 3:2-5,

I would like to learn just one thing from you: Did you receive the Spirit by observing the law, or by believing what you heard? Are you so foolish? After beginning with the Spirit, are you now trying to attain your goal by human effort? Have you suffered so much for nothing—if it really was for nothing? Does God give you his Spirit and work miracles among you because you observe the law, or because you believe what you heard?

Paul allows no lack of clarity on this, the main point of his letter to the Galatian church. Look how emphatically, how repeatedly he curses the transactional relationship with God. It is completely summed up in one phrase for Paul: the law.

But even if we or an angel from heaven should preach a gospel other than the one we preached to you, let him be eternally condemned! As we have already said, so now I say again: If anybody is preaching to you a gospel other than what you accepted, let him be eternally condemned! (1:8-9)

Yet not even Titus, who was with me, was compelled to be circumcised, even though he was a Greek. This matter arose because some false brothers had infiltrated our ranks to spy on the freedom we have in Christ Jesus and to make us slaves. We did not give in to them for a moment, so that the truth of the gospel might remain with you. (2:3-5)

When I saw that they were not acting in line with the truth of the gospel, I said to Peter in front of them all, "You are a Jew, yet you live like a Gentile and not like a Jew. How is it, then, that you force Gentiles to follow Jewish customs? We who are Jews by birth and not 'Gentile sinners' know that a man is not justified by observing the law, but by faith in Jesus Christ. So we, too, have put our faith in Christ Jesus that we may be justified by faith in Christ and not by observing the law, because by observing the law no one will be justified." (2:14-16)

All who rely on observing the law are under a curse, for it is written: "Cursed is everyone who does not continue to do everything written in the Book of the Law." Clearly no one is justified before God by the law, because, "The righteous will live by faith." The law is not based on faith; on the contrary, "The man who does these things will live by them." (3:10-12)

Before this faith came, we were held prisoners by the law, locked up until faith should be revealed. (3:23)

But now that you know God—or rather are known by God — how is it that you are turning back to those weak and miserable principles? Do you wish to be enslaved by them all over again? You are observing special days and months and seasons and years! I fear for you, that somehow I have wasted my efforts on you. (4:9-11)

In 5:2-4, Paul even condemns people in the church who promote the transactional relationship with God .

Mark my words! I, Paul, tell you that if you let yourselves be circumcised, Christ will be of no value to you at all. Again I declare to every man who lets himself be circumcised that he is obligated to obey the whole law. You who are trying to be justified by law have been alienated from Christ; you have fallen away from grace.

Paul wants you and the Galatians to enjoy the true and proper relationship with God—one based on confidence, not on transaction.

He tells us plainly that God lives in us and we have continual communion and rest with God. Listen to him in these statements.

> *I have been crucified with Christ and I no longer live, but Christ lives in me. The life I live in the body, I live by faith in the Son of God, who loved me and gave himself for me. (2:20)*

> *Christ redeemed us from the curse of the law by becoming a curse for us, for it is written: "Cursed is everyone who is hung on a tree." He redeemed us in order that the blessing given to Abraham might come to the Gentiles through Christ Jesus, so that by faith we might receive the promise of the Spirit. (3:13-14)*

Again Paul, like the other apostles, tells us that the promise of God is the filling with His Spirit. Jesus taught this plainly in John 14:15-23—

> *If you love me, you will obey what I command. And I will ask the Father, and he will give you another Counselor to be with you forever— the Spirit of truth. The world cannot accept him, because it neither sees him nor knows him. But you know him, for he lives with you and will be in you. I will not leave you as orphans; I will come to you. Before long, the world will not see me anymore, but you will see me. Because I live, you also will live. On that day you will realize that I am in my Father, and you are in me, and I am in you.*

Could "continual" be any more clear than that? Jesus immediately states the same thing again in a different way.

> *Whoever has my commands and obeys them, he is the one who loves me. He who loves me will be loved by my Father, and I too will love him and show myself to him....If anyone loves me,*

*he will obey my teaching. My Father will love him, and we will
come to him and make our home with him.*

This is the core of what you are, Christian, God the Spirit at home
in you—a confidence relationship. Paul continues to the Galatians:

*You are all sons of God through faith in Christ Jesus, for all
of you who were baptized into Christ have clothed yourselves
with Christ. There is neither Jew nor Greek, slave nor free, male
nor female, for you are all one in Christ Jesus. If you belong to
Christ, then you are Abraham's seed, and heirs according to
the promise.* (3:28-29)

*But when the time had fully come, God sent his Son, born of a
woman, born under law, to redeem those under law, that we
might receive the full rights of sons. Because you are sons, God
sent the Spirit of his Son into our hearts, the Spirit who calls
out, "Abba, Father." So you are no longer a slave, but a son;
and since you are a son, God has made you also an heir.* (4:4-7)

*Now you, brothers, like Isaac, are children of promise. At that
time the son born in the ordinary way persecuted the son born
by the power of the Spirit. It is the same now. But what does
the Scripture say? "Get rid of the slave woman and her son, for
the slave woman's son will never share in the inheritance with
the free woman's son." Therefore, brothers, we are not children
of the slave woman, but of the free woman.* (4:28-31)

*But by faith we eagerly await through the Spirit the
righteousness for which we hope. For in Christ Jesus neither
circumcision nor uncircumcision has any value. The only thing
that counts is faith expressing itself through love.* (5:5-6)

So I say, live by the Spirit, and you will not gratify the desires of the sinful nature. For the sinful nature desires what is contrary to the Spirit, and the Spirit what is contrary to the sinful nature. They are in conflict with each other, so that you do not do what you want. But if you are led by the Spirit, you are not under law. (5:16-18)

Since we live by the Spirit, let us keep in step with the Spirit. (5:25)

Do not be deceived: God cannot be mocked. A man reaps what he sows. The one who sows to please his sinful nature, from that nature will reap destruction; the one who sows to please the Spirit, from the Spirit will reap eternal life. (6:8)

The last one is conditional, but not based on following a code. You can opt out of continual communion with God by pleasing your flesh, and your results will show that choice. You can make a choice not to please the Spirit, and to stay blindfolded. Yes, He is continual and constant, but this is not a permission slip for you to be whimsical or flighty toward Him. As Hebrews 10:30-31 tells us sternly,

For we know him who said, "It is mine to avenge; I will repay," and again, "The Lord will judge his people." It is a dreadful thing to fall into the hands of the living God.

Is it not much more appealing to enjoy a constant and continual communion with God? Pleasing our flesh is beset with the laws of diminishing returns, but in communion with God are joys forevermore. *But we are not of those who shrink back and are destroyed, but of those who believe and are saved.* (Hebrews 10:39) The identity He has given you with all its privileges is a much better way to live. Who would prefer blindfolds to that?

ACTIVATION 6-3

We end with activations. Their purpose is for you to yield to the truths you have seen here. Answer the following as if the Scriptures are true—you do indeed have a confidence relationship with God regardless of your awareness.

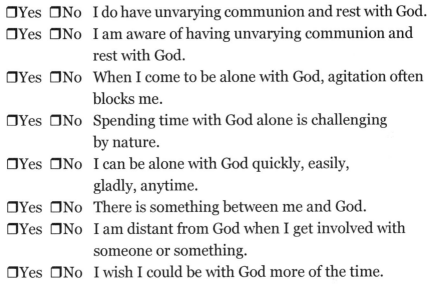

☐Yes ☐No I do have unvarying communion and rest with God.

☐Yes ☐No I am aware of having unvarying communion and rest with God.

☐Yes ☐No When I come to be alone with God, agitation often blocks me.

☐Yes ☐No Spending time with God alone is challenging by nature.

☐Yes ☐No I can be alone with God quickly, easily, gladly, anytime.

☐Yes ☐No There is something between me and God.

☐Yes ☐No I am distant from God when I get involved with someone or something.

☐Yes ☐No I wish I could be with God more of the time.

Your answers now, after this truth soaking into you, should be different from the answers you gave in Activation One.

ACTIVATION 6-4

I mentioned hymns earlier, a big part of our life. In any given moment, each of the hymns below fits perfectly and we sing them with true intent from the relationship we have with God, transactional or confidence. Check the following song words as transactional (T) or confidence (C) by the way you might sing them, a subjective window on your own outlook. Some are hymns, some are choruses, and some are antique. If you're unsure, you can look them up online for all the words.

☐ T ☐ C We are hungry for more of You, we are thirsty for more of You, I need more of You.

☐ T ☐ C   Just as I am, without one plea, but that Thy blood was shed for me

☐ T ☐ C   Shepherd, Your sheep are weary. We need to hear Your voice, we just need to hear it.

☐ T ☐ C   This is the air I breathe, Your holy presence.

☐ T ☐ C   We lift our voices higher and higher to You.

☐ T ☐ C   I once was lost but now am found, was blind but now I see.

☐ T ☐ C   The Lord hears my prayers & answers them; He bends down & listens.

☐ T ☐ C   I love You Lord, & I lift my voice, to worship you; o my soul, rejoice, Take joy....

☐ T ☐ C   Draw me nearer, nearer, nearer Blessed Lord to Thy precious bleeding side.

☐ T ☐ C   As the deer panteth for the water, so my soul longeth after thee.

☐ T ☐ C   Every move I make, I make in You. Every breath I take, I breathe in You.

☐ T ☐ C   We wait for you to walk in the room.

ACTIVATION 6-5

☐Yes ☐No   I am second-class compared to my church leadership.

☐Yes ☐No   The people I look up to are closer to God than I am.

☐Yes ☐No   God is more powerful in more mature Christians than He is in me.

☐Yes ☐No   To get my prayers answered, I need stronger Christians to pray for me.

☐Yes ☐No   The way to feel close to God is in worship, evangelism, service or some type of Christian ministry.

☐Yes ☐No   I look forward to being a better Christian.

Brother, sister, you already are each of those. Your answer should be NO to each one because they are transactional!

ACTIVATION 6-6

☐Yes ☐No No matter what happens, I am safe.

☐Yes ☐No When I sin, God is farther away.

☐Yes ☐No Nothing can get closer to me than He is.

☐Yes ☐No Worship brings God closer to me.

☐Yes ☐No The Holy Spirit lives in me constantly, superior to all my problems.

☐Yes ☐No The best way to put yourself at ease is to do something for God.

☐Yes ☐No God never stops loving and favoring me.

If this chapter is true, and if you can accept it, the answer pattern there is yes, no, alternating.

What are you, Christian? You are a new creature, with spiritual perception, one of a new race of men, Spirit-born, who is in continual communion and rest with your Creator.

Holy Spirit, thank you for declaring Jesus' truths to me,
and for removing my old blindfolds.
I appreciate my rest in You.

CHAPTER 7:
YOU ARE A FULLY EQUIPPED RULER, RULING BY YOUR WILL & YOUR WORDS, WHOSE RULERSHIP POSITION IS READY FOR YOUR MATURITY

ACTIVATION 7-1

Imagine for a moment that you rule the earth, and you have all power and authority on earth, second only to God. What would you decree?

1. _____
2. _____
3. _____

Pretend now that your rule extends to heaven as well as earth—that you have all power and authority in the heavenly realms as well as earth, second only to God. Now what do you decree?

1. _____
2. _____
3. _____

What would be next after these?

1. _____
2. _____
3. _____

Christians and churches worldwide are awakening to God's stated purpose that we rule earth for Him, a purpose He clearly stated at our original creation in Genesis 1:26 & 28.

> *Let us make man in our image, in our likeness, and let them rule over the fish of the sea and the birds of the air, over the livestock, over all the earth, and over all the creatures that move along the ground." ...God blessed them and said to them,*

"Be fruitful and increase in number; fill the earth and subdue it. Rule over the fish of the sea and the birds of the air and over every living creature that moves on the ground.

As with any new learning, the students have accidents and misunderstandings, and God's saints today are no exception.

When I was learning to drive, I gashed my Dad's Chevrolet Caprice all the way from front to back—with him witnessing the entire slow torture from the passenger seat. He was mad. Mad! But after a few days to cool down, and a lot of conversation, I was back in the driver's seat and he was back in the passenger seat. He still wanted me to drive. He was confident that I could, so much so he didn't even buckle his seat belt.

Same with our Father. He still wants us to drive. Despite all the stumbles and failures in His church's attempts to rule politically, or behaviorally, or morally, or economically, He still wants us to drive and is confident we can. We are after all the Spirit-born, in the image of His Son. He hasn't rescinded any of the ruler's promises in the Scripture. He still authorizes and expects us to rule in prayer and other ways—even desiring us to.

Yet as intent and resolute as He is that we saints shall rule the earth for Him, we presently see very limited rulership from people who follow Jesus. It's important to recognize regional differences exist, for where the gospel is expanding in the earth, there are always many powerful deeds by His church. But in America, for instance, are we seeing such rulership as this in Mark 4:39-41?

He got up, rebuked the wind and said to the waves, "Quiet! Be still!" Then the wind died down and it was completely calm. He said to his disciples, "Why are you so afraid? Do you still have no faith?" They were terrified and asked each other, "Who is this? Even the wind and the waves obey him!"

Where is the new normal, the manifestation daily of our rulership?

As much as my dad wanted me to drive, he wouldn't teach me until the right time. At least I had to see over the dashboard, and reach the brake pedal.

Our Father generally withholds our rulership and waits until we are ready before He releases us to it. The position of rulership is decreed and waits for your maturity. God habitually withholds things until the right time, as we saw in earlier chapters.

So in the Kingdom of our God, what readiness does He seek? What signs of maturity equate to seeing over the dashboard as a spiritual being? The Scripture is full of answers kept from us, answers we haven't understood as maturity-inducing statements.

Remember what James said in 4:2-5, that while we were materialistic and transactional, we were vulnerable to misusing our rulership. Like the two on the road to Emmaus, we *were kept from recognizing Him.* (Luke 24:16) The revelation of Scripture is so plain once you perceive it, the only explanation for not seeing it is God's keeping for the right time, our maturity.

Now however is the time. It appears God has withdrawn all permission for His church to maintain its immaturity. He is unwilling to continue indulging our willful blindness to our mandated authority. He said earth shall be ruled by us. His resolve is strong, the momentum of spiritual perception is gathering speed, and those who will not yield are revealed not to be poor in spirit.

Events globally bear out this reading of our time. Missionaries and authors report that Christians throughout the world are manifesting great power and authority like Jesus. In America itself, powerful schools and seminars are effectively training Christians to exert their will in concert with the will of God. Christians and churches who won't yield their ear to the Spirit of God are falling in attendance, laying off staff due to low collections, and closing their doors.

Jesus Himself set this new accountability in motion and it was evident even in His infancy. When Simeon met Joseph and Mary in the Temple, he described that Jesus would reveal what a person is within. He prophesied over Jesus in Luke 2:34-35.

> *Then Simeon blessed them and said to Mary, his mother: "This child is destined to cause the falling and rising of many in Israel, and to be a sign that will be spoken against, so that the thoughts of many hearts will be revealed.*

So what is our rulership?

Sometimes it is easier to define something by what it is not than by what it is. The activation to start this chapter played that purpose. Don't fall under accusation for any of your answers, as you become aware of God's way of removing your blindfold.

You see, there actually was someone who had all authority in heaven and on earth, second only to God. This person was the highest angel—Lucifer. God himself says so in Ezekiel 28:11-14, figured in Ezekiel's contemporary the king of Tyre, & clearly descriptive of Lucifer.

> *This is what the Sovereign LORD says:*

> *"'You were the model of perfection,*
>   *full of wisdom and perfect in beauty.*
> *You were in Eden,*
>   *the garden of God;*
> *every precious stone adorned you:*
>   *ruby, topaz and emerald,*
>   *chrysolite, onyx and jasper,*
>   *sapphire, turquoise and beryl.*
> *Your settings and mountings were made of gold;*
>   *on the day you were created they were prepared.*
> *You were anointed as a guardian cherub,*

for so I ordained you.
You were on the holy mount of God;
* you walked among the fiery stones.*
You were blameless in your ways
* from the day you were created..."*

If an archangel in the very presence of God can't rule, how can you? A poor in spirit person may remember the activation answers at the first of the chapter with a little embarrassment now.

God tells us what went wrong, both in Ezekiel 28:15-17 and in Isaiah 14:12-15, where the king of Assyria is the figure used for statements that clearly exceed any man's qualities.

"...till wickedness was found in you.
Through your widespread trade
* you were filled with violence,*
* and you sinned.*
So I drove you in disgrace from the mount of God,
* and I expelled you, O guardian cherub,*
* from among the fiery stones.*
Your heart became proud
* on account of your beauty,*
and you corrupted your wisdom
* because of your splendor.*
So I threw you to the earth;
* I made a spectacle of you before kings.*
By your many sins and dishonest trade
* you have desecrated your sanctuaries.*

How you have fallen from heaven,
* O morning star, son of the dawn!*
You have been cast down to the earth,
* you who once laid low the nations!*
You said in your heart,
* "I will ascend to heaven;*

I will raise my throne
   above the stars of God;
I will sit enthroned on the mount of assembly,
   on the utmost heights of the sacred mountain.
I will ascend above the tops of the clouds;
   I will make myself like the Most High."

Think of what Lucifer's flaw damaged in the ideal purposes of God. One third of the angels (Revelation 12:4); the entire earth itself (Revelation 12:9,12); and His entire new race of earth-rulers (II Corinthians 4:4, Revelation 12:9).

What was the wickedness found in Lucifer? "Your heart became proud" in Ezekiel 28. Through Isaiah, God further describes the fault found in Lucifer: his jealousy of God's rulership and pride to exalt himself over God. *I will ascend, I will raise my throne, I will sit enthroned, I will ascend, <u>I will make myself like the Most High</u>.*

Even our good desires—our miracles, our prophesying, our driving out demons—turn luciferian if we allow in ourselves the same wickedness of "I will." My problem and yours is this: we can't *not* allow it. We were spiritually dead, and we are poor in spirit still. Spirit-born, yet so unequal to it. The Christian who rejoices in our pending rulership, who easily lists what he or she shall do when fully released, is in danger of luciferian pride.

Praise God! He has provided His people with a birthright solution so simple that this danger is easily avoided: poverty of spirit mourned, meekness and hunger with thirsting for righteousness. Those are obviously, completely, non-luciferian qualities. When present, these qualities inoculate us against the luciferian infection.

If our readiness for rulership is signaled by our poverty of spirit and by the consequent qualities that Jesus listed in the Beatitudes, how do these qualities manifest and evidence themselves in one of God's rulers like you and me? Let's turn our attention to this practical question and equip ourselves with full resolve to mature into rulership.

How do you rule if you are poor in spirit, mourning, meek, and so forth?

The Scripture answers this question perhaps more than any other single question of how to live. Our list is only introductory! Let's begin with Jesus, described by Paul in Philippians 2:4-8.

Do nothing out of selfish ambition or vain conceit, but in humility consider others better than yourselves. Each of you should look not only to your own interests, but also to the interests of others. Your attitude should be the same as that of Christ Jesus:

Who, being in very nature God,
  did not consider equality with God something to be grasped,
but made himself nothing,
  taking the very nature of a servant,
  being made in human likeness.
And being found in appearance as a man,
  he humbled himself
  and became obedient to death —
    even death on a cross!

The luciferian "I will" is disarmed by such behavior. This poverty of spirit humility and yieldedness is God's signal of our ability to see over the dashboard, of our readiness to learn how to drive. Look how the Father responds to Jesus' taking on our poverty of spirit:

Therefore God exalted him to the highest place
  and gave him the name that is above every name,
that at the name of Jesus every knee should bow,
  in heaven and on earth and under the earth,
and every tongue confess that Jesus Christ is Lord,
  to the glory of God the Father.

Jesus taught this luciferian antidote repeatedly. Luke 13:29-30 concludes his answer to how many people will be saved.

People will come from east and west and north and south, and will take their places at the feast in the kingdom of God. Indeed there are those who are last who will be first, and first who will be last.

He repeats it again to religious people who honored themselves by the seats they chose at table, Luke 14:11.

For everyone who exalts himself will be humbled, and he who humbles himself will be exalted.

Luciferian pride often shows up in religion and Jesus expressed the antidote of poverty of spirit from that perspective as well, in Luke 15:7 and in 18:13-14, a well-known parable.

I tell you that in the same way there will be more rejoicing in heaven over one sinner who repents than over ninety-nine righteous persons who do not need to repent.

But the tax collector stood at a distance. He would not even look up to heaven, but beat his breast and said, 'God, have mercy on me, a sinner.' I tell you that this man, rather than the other, went home justified before God. For everyone who exalts himself will be humbled, and he who humbles himself will be exalted.

Don't feel bad if you haven't appreciated this repeated teaching as the antidote to luciferian disqualification. Don't blame your teachers for not understanding its importance. Neither did the disciples who heard it directly for three years. Consider Mark 9:33-35, where Jesus

...asked them, "What were you arguing about on the road?"
But they kept quiet because on the way they had argued about
who was the greatest. Sitting down, Jesus called the Twelve
and said, "If anyone wants to be first, he must be the very last,
and the servant of all."

Let's have mercy on the ones who don't understand this because
we have been slow also—and so were the disciples. James and John
approached it in a goofy way in Mark 10:35, and Jesus' reply in
10:43-45 contains the antidote of humility and poverty of spirit yet
again.

Then James and John, the sons of Zebedee, came to him.
"Teacher," they said, "we want you to do for us whatever we
ask." "What do you want me to do for you?" he asked. They
replied, "Let one of us sit at your right and the other at your
left in your glory."
Jesus replied..."Whoever wants to become great among
you must be your servant, and whoever wants to be first must
be slave of all. For even the Son of Man did not come to be
served, but to serve, and to give his life as a ransom for many."

Jesus taught this even up to the last night of His life. At what He
knew and we now know to have been the Last Supper—but not the
disciples—listen to what He said in Luke 22:26-27.

The greatest among you should be like the youngest, and the
one who rules like the one who serves. For who is greater, the
one who is at the table or the one who serves? Is it not the one
who is at the table? But I am among you as one who serves.

And what results when we follow His example? Jesus' very next
statement says what. As the Father has promised Him, so Jesus
promises us, His future earth-rulers:

You are those who have stood by me in my trials. And I confer on you a kingdom, just as my Father conferred one on me, so that you may eat and drink at my table in my kingdom and sit on thrones, judging the twelve tribes of Israel. (Luke 22:28-30)

Naturally you may wonder, "if I am serving, humbling myself, lowering myself, and exalting others, serving others, how can rulership take place?"

Let's pull together what we have seen so far. As God reveals in Daniel 7:27, it remains His intention that the saints shall rule His kingdom.

Then the sovereignty, power and greatness of the kingdoms under the whole heaven will be handed over to the saints, the people of the Most High. His kingdom will be an everlasting kingdom, and all rulers will worship and obey him.

And who are you, saint? You are a follower of Jesus who holds nothing back from Him. You are a saint who says goodbye to everything you value, for His sake. You are spiritually perceptive so you can function in the heavenly realm as well as earthly. You are an undeserving beloved of this wonderful Father. You are one of a new race of men, born of the Spirit, living as people Spirit-dominant, and filled with God who has made His home in you. You are His new creature, in unvarying communion and rest with your Creator, freed from transactional into confidence relationship with Him. And now we are considering your identity as a fully equipped ruler, ruling by your will and words, from a position into which you are maturing even as you read.

Of ourselves we are poor in spirit, mourning, meek and hungry. Such people allow all the rulership to be expressed by God's initiative in them.

You have a will, like every created person has eternally and independently. When you become filled with the Spirit of God and

He makes His home in you, a new will comes to function within you, alongside your will. That is His will.

Which will is superior?

Jesus taught and demonstrated how we rule: *Thy will be done*. It comes from the Lord's prayer in Matthew 6:9-13, elegant for its simplicity and childlike authority.

> *Our Father in heaven, hallowed be your name.*
> *Your kingdom come, your will be done on earth as it is in*
> *heaven.*
> *Give us today our daily bread.*
> *Forgive us our debts, as we also have forgiven our debtors.*
> *And lead us not into temptation, but deliver us from the evil*
> *one.'*

Sometimes we think like stereotypical glamor contestants when we read or say *Thy will be done*. We identify it with world peace, or feeding the poor, or being nice and getting along, or even letting loved ones go when our prayer for their recovery is unanswered.

This is not at all how Jesus spoke of God's will being done. Instead, Jesus showed us that praying *Thy will be done* refers to a moment-by-moment decision of our spirit to yield our will to His will who lives in us. Put another way, Jesus made a moment-by-moment decision to have no luciferian "I will" in him, and has enabled us to do the same.

Jesus demonstrated this in His actions, John 5:19—

> *the Son can do nothing by himself; he can do only what he sees*
> *his Father doing, because whatever the Father does the Son*
> *also does.*

He demonstrated it in His judging, John 5:22,27 & 30.

the Father judges no one, but has entrusted all judgment to the Son....He [the Father] has given him authority to judge because he is the Son of Man. ...By myself I can do nothing; I judge only as I hear, and my judgment is just, for I seek not to please myself but him who sent me.

Imagine Jesus, sinless Son of God and Son of Man, withholding judgment on those around Him. I could not have. Consider John 8:26, 28.

I have much to say in judgment of you. But he who sent me is reliable, and what I have heard from him I tell the world....I do nothing on my own but speak just what the Father has taught me.

And as for speech, He showed us that our tongue (and the mind behind it) can be yielded to God in each moment prior to speaking. Jesus said so in John 12:49-50.

For I did not speak of my own accord, but the Father who sent me commanded me what to say and how to say it. I know that his command leads to eternal life. So whatever I say is just what the Father has told me to say.

We saw in earlier chapters the passage in which Jesus explains how he cursed the fig tree. He applied the same principle to you and me and each believer. In Mark 11:23-24, He says,

if anyone says to this mountain, 'Go, throw yourself into the sea,' and does not doubt in his heart but believes that what he says will happen, it will be done for him. Therefore I tell you, whatever you ask for in prayer, believe that you have received it, and it will be yours.

But what is the principle that He expands and applies to us as the foundation of this power? 11:22,

"Have faith in God," Jesus answered.

Clearly by this Jesus isn't specifying a transaction quantity, but a confidence quality. Where many prayers based on self-confidence in one's faith have gone unanswered, every such decree made in shared confidence has its source in the Superior Will that resides in you and me.

Jesus taught us to pray, *Thy will be done.* He instructed us *to have faith in God.* So how do we rule? We obey what God says. We restrict ourselves to will only what He and we will together.

Micah 6:8 states this beautifully.

He has showed you, O man, what is good.
And what does the LORD require of you?
To act justly and to love mercy
and to walk humbly with your God.

You may well be confused. If you are to be God's ruler on earth, together with all His saints, if you are poor in Spirit yet Spirit-born, if you are servant of all, if you are giving your will back to God and letting His superior will dominate within you, what does your rule look like?

You rule with your will and your words. The Bible gives you a picture of it in the Lord's Prayer—*Thy will be* done (Matthew 6:9). The Greek word which in English becomes *Thy will be done* is transliterated *genestheto*. That word is also used in the Greek translation of the Old Testament from Hebrew, called the "Septuagint" and completed prior to Jesus' time. We see *genestheto* in Genesis 1 where God created everything—*Let there be light.*

There you see rulership occurring by will and words.

We read in Genesis 2:15 that God put man in the garden *to work it and take care of it.* We think of hoeing and raking, perhaps. But how was the concept of work introduced in Scripture? By God's work of creating by will and words as in Genesis 2:2-3.

> *By the seventh day God had finished the work he had been doing; so on the seventh day he rested from all his work. And God blessed the seventh day and made it holy, because on it he rested from all the work of creating that he had done.*

And our next exposure to work is? The work of the man in the garden. So the pattern of work, for a creature who was just created in the image and likeness of God, is more likely the way God worked, not the way we identify work today. Agreed?

And that work is by will and by words. So what was our first work of caring for the garden? Not hoeing and raking, but naming—naming the animals and the woman.

That further explains an otherwise strange statement and action by God in Genesis 11:6-7.

> *The LORD said, "If as one people speaking the same language they have begun to do this, then nothing they plan to do will be impossible for them. Come, let us go down and confuse their language so they will not understand each other."*

Because words are such a critical element in all God does, and because we are in His image, our words are therefore an equally critical element of all that we do. Therefore God's solution in this passage was to confuse our language. That event is known as Babel, from which we get our English word, *babble.* God's purpose there was to handicap the effectiveness of mankind's words—important to our coming considerations.

Notice God's own assessment of our capabilities: *Nothing will be impossible for them.* That is quite a statement coming from our Creator.

Jesus chose this principle—ruling by will and words—to introduce Himself when he chose Isaiah 61:1-2 to read in His first synagogue invitation, related in Luke 4:17-19.

The scroll of the prophet Isaiah was handed to him. Unrolling it, he found the place where it is written:

The Spirit of the Lord is on me,
    because he has anointed me
    to preach good news to the poor.
He has sent me to proclaim freedom for the prisoners
    and recovery of sight for the blind,
to release the oppressed,
to proclaim the year of the Lord's favor.

Notice: it's verbal activity with a result that changes all of a person's life. Ruling by will and words.

And history shows that we know this as a race of men. All of our stumblings to greatness have relied upon the will of key people. From an idea in their head, they ruled others with their words. Sadly, the same is true of our descent to evil, where people are ruled by the words of charismatic criminals. Friedrich Nietzsche, atheistic existentialist philosopher in the late 1800s, wrote of the Superman who ruled by his will and his words to apply natural selection for achieving the creation of a super race—chillingly prophetic of the Nazi horror.

It's in our movies too. Action movies are a platform of physical near-invincibility on which to display the strong will of the protagonist. Trauma movies are a platform of near-complete vulnerability to display the impaired and weak will. And these dramas exist because we relate to them, enabling the advertising and ticket sales to support their production.

If our work is by will and by words, it makes much more sense of some hard-to-understand statements Jesus made. In them, the underlying fact is the effective power of our will and our words. Here are just a few from Matthew—pay attention to the verbal activity of all the verbs.

Anyone who says to his brother, 'Raca,' is answerable to the Sanhedrin. But anyone who says, 'You fool!' will be in danger of the fire of hell. (5:22)

But I tell you, Do not swear at all: either by heaven, for it is God's throne; or by the earth, for it is his footstool; or by Jerusalem, for it is the city of the Great King. And do not swear by your head, for you cannot make even one hair white or black. Simply let your 'Yes' be 'Yes,' and your 'No,' 'No'; anything beyond this comes from the evil one. (5:34-36)

When you enter a house, first say, 'Peace to this house.' If a man of peace is there, your peace will rest on him; if not, it will return to you. (Luke 10:5-6)

You brood of vipers, how can you who are evil say anything good? For out of the overflow of the heart the mouth speaks. The good man brings good things out of the good stored up in him, and the evil man brings evil things out of the evil stored up in him. But I tell you that men will have to give account on the day of judgment for every careless word they have spoken. For by your words you will be acquitted, and by your words you will be condemned. (12:34-37)

Jesus called the crowd to him and said, "Listen and understand. What goes into a man's mouth does not make him 'unclean,' but what comes out of his mouth, that is what makes him 'unclean.'" (15:10-11)

I will give you the keys of the kingdom of heaven; whatever you bind on earth will be bound in heaven, and whatever you loose on earth will be loosed in heaven. (16:19)

If you have faith as small as a mustard seed, you can say to this mountain, 'Move from here to there' and it will move. Nothing will be impossible for you. (17:20)

Jesus knew this to be true of Himself. Consider John 6:63 & 15:3.

The Spirit gives life; the flesh counts for nothing. The words I have spoken to you are spirit and they are life.
   You are already clean because of the word I have spoken to you.

Of course, where you see asking and praying, you now will see it as a subset of that ruling by will and words. Like Mark 11:22-24 above, Jesus says we can have whatever we ask or pray.

So I say to you: Ask and it will be given to you; seek and you will find; knock and the door will be opened to you. For everyone who asks receives; he who seeks finds; and to him who knocks, the door will be opened. Which of you fathers, if your son asks for a fish, will give him a snake instead? Or if he asks for an egg, will give him a scorpion? If you then, though you are evil, know how to give good gifts to your children, how much more will your Father in heaven give the Holy Spirit to those who ask him! (Luke 11:9-13)

Anyone who has faith in me will do what I have been doing. He will do even greater things than these, because I am going to the Father. And I will do whatever you ask in my name, so that the Son may bring glory to the Father. You may ask me for anything in my name, and I will do it. (John 14:12-13)

If you remain in me and my words remain in you, ask whatever you wish and it will be given you. (John 15:7)

Jesus and the NT writers make such statements many times. They must have meant it. Asking is an important and childlike way that we Christians rule by our will and our words. Truly one sign of our poverty of spirit is that it takes so much effort sometimes simply to ask God a question. One sign of the luciferian infection is how readily we think we can do it ourselves and don't need to ask.

This fact—that you, Christian, are a fully equipped ruler, ruling by your will and your words—explains something in the New Testament that has proven hard to grasp for some Christians:

What is speaking in tongues all about?

Think of it. It wasn't prominent in the Old Testament. No NT author recorded that Jesus gave any prior instruction about it. It comes down to this: The Holy Spirit was poured out to remain in us, and boom! We're speaking in tongues. What is that all about? Of all the possible signs He could have chosen, why that one? If you shun attention or are in a more traditional denomination, you might ask, why something so embarrassing?

But we know within there has to be some reason, right? If you are a true follower of Jesus, you do not ignore it for one second. This is what He did. He did it for a good reason. As Lord of you, He expects you to receive what He sent. Any deviation betrays an area where we are unwilling to say goodbye to all we hold dear and unwilling to elevate Him to our dearest. Embarrassment over something God has done is a red flag signaling danger in our own heart.

It quickly becomes evident why the Spirit's filling was married to speaking in tongues, when you think about the prominence of our tongue from what James says in James 3:2,5-7.

> *If anyone is never at fault in what he says, he is a perfect man, able to keep his whole body in check. ...the tongue is a small part of the body, but it makes great boasts. Consider what a great forest is set on fire by a small spark. The tongue also is a fire, a world of evil among the parts of the body. It corrupts the whole person, sets the whole course of his life on fire, and is itself set on fire by hell. All kinds of animals, birds, reptiles and creatures of the sea are being tamed and have been tamed by man, but no man can tame the tongue. It is a restless evil, full of deadly poison.*

This being our situation, we are reduced to poverty of spirit once again. As Jesus said above, *You brood of vipers, how can you who are evil say anything good?* Truly this causes us to mourn— something so central to us, being so irreparably polluted. James continues in 3:9-12,

> *With the tongue we praise our Lord and Father, and with it we curse men, who have been made in God's likeness. Out of the same mouth come praise and cursing. My brothers, this should not be. Can both fresh water and salt water flow from the same spring? My brothers, can a fig tree bear olives, or a grapevine bear figs? Neither can a salt spring produce fresh water.*

What can be done for our tongue? Just this: when God makes His home in us, when the Holy Spirit lives in us, He remedies the pollution of our tongue by giving us a new language. We are Spirit-born, and it makes sense to me that we also have a language that is born of the Spirit.

To whom is the language directed? It is directed to God, as Paul says in I Corinthians 14:2,

For anyone who speaks in a tongue does not speak to men but to God. Indeed, no one understands him; he utters mysteries with his spirit.

Speaking in tongues is a great sign of our rulership. We will to yield our tongue to the Holy Spirit. He is always communicating. With Him, we will to speak in tongues, and it is in words. It is the words of God living in us, as if our mouth and lips and tongue are dominated by the agreement of our will and His who lives in us.

Think about it. There are two wills living in your body now, if you are a Spirit-born follower of Jesus. Of the two wills, one is superior and one is inferior. Who gets to run the show of your life? Amazingly, God, the superior will in you, defers to your decision on that matter. If you decide that He runs your show, and if you give Him your capacity of will and of words for the use of His will, then He will do so. And if not, then He will let you run your show. In either case, you reap what you sow. All of us can say, our sowing isn't as good as His sowing that occurs when His superior will is running our show.

One of the tremendous benefits of speaking in tongues regularly is the practice of submitting our tongue and all our verbal faculties. There is a practice of moment-by-moment submission that is bound up inextricably with speaking in tongues. Do you want to be more yielded to God, more continually? Then speak in tongues continually. It is a practice of yielding continually. Quietly or loudly, calmly or actively, in every way—all kinds of prayers, just as Paul instructed the Ephesians in 6:18—

And pray in the Spirit on all occasions with all kinds of prayers and requests. With this in mind, be alert and always keep on praying for all the saints.

There are over 70 benefits described in Scripture for speaking in tongues. When you are ready to explore them, get the book *70 Reasons for Speaking in Tongues* by Bishop Bill Hamon of Christian International.

But one other purpose of speaking in tongues belongs here. It directly applies to our chapter's subject, that you are a fully equipped ruler ruling by your will and your words.

Speaking in tongues is a reversal of God's intent at the Tower of Babel to handicap our effectiveness. Speaking in tongues undoes Babel's confusion. Where God regarded the effectiveness of men's speech as something to be handicapped, He now opens heaven to the influence of our words. What men sought to obtain by building a tower, He freely gives by placing the speech of His Spirit into the mouths of His Spirit-born saints.

This is why Paul in I Corinthians 13:1—often cited erroneously as a rationalization for abandoning speaking in tongues—describes it this way:

> *If I speak in the tongues of men and of angels, but have not love, I am only a resounding gong or a clanging cymbal.*

The misuse of their spiritual gifts by the Corinthians doesn't justify throwing out the baby with the bathwater. The gifts are given and are without respect for the believer's maturity. Paul said to the Corinthians, notorious for their immaturity,

> *For in him you have been enriched in every way—in all your speaking and in all your knowledge—because our testimony about Christ was confirmed in you. Therefore you do not lack any spiritual gift as you eagerly wait for our Lord Jesus Christ to be revealed.* (I Corinthians 1:5-7)

Maturity results when the fruit of the Spirit—love, joy, peace, patience, gentleness, self-control & the others from Galatians 5:22—are grown over time. Gifts are given, but fruit is grown. How many examples do we have—too many—of Christians whose gifts catapulted them to a prominence unmatched by their character? To a fame unmatched by the fruit of the Spirit in them?

Lucifer had mighty gifts—gifts that exceeded his character. The evidently Christian people who are judged in Matthew 7:20-21 had mighty gifts—gifts that were not matched with poverty of spirit.

Speaking in tongues can be like playing with fire. And that is exactly what He said He came to do—to baptize us with fire and with the Holy Spirit. For many, the dilemma is like David's when the ark seemed too hot to handle and Uzzah was killed (II Samuel 6). But it is a dilemma only if we don't listen to God about it—which David did. The dilemma was remedied easily in I Chronicles 15:13.

If He is Lord and if you are His follower, you are fully equipped to rule by your will and your words. When you see yourself biblically, when you trust His decree of what you are and can do, then you are free from domination by a fear of failing that keeps you ineffective. Hebrews 10:39 exhorts,

> *we are not of those who shrink back and are destroyed, but of those who believe and are saved.*

Jesus warned in Luke 9:62,

> *No one who puts his hand to the plow and looks back is fit for service in the kingdom of God.*

Instead, He expected his follower to have this response:

> *From the days of John the Baptist until now, the kingdom of heaven has been forcefully advancing, and forceful men lay hold of it.* (Matthew 11:12)

Walking humbly with our God doesn't mean passivity. Meekness doesn't mean timidity. If forceful men lay hold of the kingdom, then poor-in-spirit people are to be forceful. Meek people are to be forceful.

Being last is not a bottom-of-the-barrel status. It is having a healthy and free acceptance of our poverty of spirit, responding accordingly. In this then, our forcefulness consists of assertiveness in repentance, of forcefulness in being meek.

In truth, so great were we originally made, and so polluted through sin is our will, that it takes the strongest strength to yield to anything we can't manipulate. Not to mention, yielding to God.

Apostle Paul demonstrates forceful yieldedness repeatedly. Here is his resolute will when he came to Corinth originally, described in I Corinthians 2:1-3.

When I came to you, brothers, I did not come with eloquence or superior wisdom as I proclaimed to you the testimony about God. For I resolved to know nothing while I was with you except Jesus Christ and him crucified. I came to you in weakness and fear, and with much trembling.

Their immaturity requires Paul to call attention to his attitude of resolute meekness in I Corinthians 9:19,22-23 & 27.

Though I am free and belong to no man, I make myself a slave to everyone, to win as many as possible....I have become all things to all men so that by all possible means I might save some. I do all this for the sake of the gospel, that I may share in its blessings. ...I beat my body and make it my slave so that after I have preached to others, I myself will not be disqualified for the prize.

When the Corinthians' resolve to be immature requires a second letter, Paul uses his own example to exemplify forceful resignation to his thorn in the flesh, in II Corinthians 12:9-10.

But he [God] said to me, "My grace is sufficient for you, for my power is made perfect in weakness. " Therefore I will boast all the more gladly about my weaknesses, so that Christ's power may rest on me. That is why, for Christ's sake, I delight in weaknesses, in insults, in hardships, in persecutions, in difficulties. For when I am weak, then I am strong.

What are you, Christian? You are a fully equipped ruler. You rule by your will and your words. Your position awaits your maturity.

Activation time. Remember our first activation this chapter? Well, you actually have been given power and authority in heaven and on earth. Jesus said it in Matthew 16:19. Is Jesus talking about physically handcuffing spiritual beings? No, of course not.

I will give you the keys of the kingdom of heaven; whatever you bind on earth will be bound in heaven, and whatever you loose on earth will be loosed in heaven.

ACTIVATION 7-2

What do you and your race have keys to? List examples of what we bind, and of what we loose.

_____

_____

_____

_____

ACTIVATION 7-3

Check the person(s) you think could comfortably make each of the following statements. Think about what you've just read! *Hint:* They all start with "I will."

❏Lucifer ❏Jesus   I will do what God says.

❏Lucifer ❏Jesus   I will evangelize and lead many people to faith.

❏Lucifer ❏Jesus   I will obey the authorities in my life.

☐Lucifer ☐Jesus   I will make my church read this book.

☐Lucifer ☐Jesus   I will verify with God what I think He is putting on my heart.

☐Lucifer ☐Jesus   I will help someone I know to understand these things.

☐Lucifer ☐Jesus   I will not act on my own, God helping me.

☐Lucifer ☐Jesus   I will make sure I have what I need.

☐Lucifer ☐Jesus   I will yield to what God has called me to do.

☐Lucifer ☐Jesus   I will not deal with the person who is so difficult for me.

☐Lucifer ☐Jesus   I will submit to the needs of those around me, as God directs.

I know those were challenging to discern. Remember Jesus' multiple warnings that doing good things is not a preventive from the luciferian "I will." The resolve that is approved for us is the forceful resolve to yield to God. Therefore the answers above begin with **JESUS** and alternate to the last one which is **JESUS**.

What are you, Christian? And equally as important in this chapter, what are you *not*?

Lord Jesus, thank you for removing the blindfold
so I can see Your rulership purpose for my existence.
Your will be done! May I so rule, that it is.

CHAPTER 8:
YOU ARE AN ESSENTIAL EXPRESSION OF GOD'S LOVE FOR PEOPLE, AND A MINISTER IN THE CHURCH, HIS ETERNAL BRIDE

Until now we haven't discussed many customary Christian concepts. One of these is fellowship. We've waited because for your fellowship to be any good, you have to know what kind of fellow you are, and what Fellow lives in you. This is what we have been doing so far.

This chapter is necessary because everything you have read about yourself has its origin in Jesus' love for His Eternal Bride. Listen to what God showed John, so we could feel His intimate longing for us His Bride, in Revelation 21:2-5.

> *I saw the Holy City, the new Jerusalem, coming down out of heaven from God, prepared as a bride beautifully dressed for her husband. And I heard a loud voice from the throne saying, "Now the dwelling of God is with men, and he will live with them. They will be his people, and God himself will be with them and be their God. He will wipe every tear from their eyes. There will be no more death or mourning or crying or pain, for the old order of things has passed away." He who was seated on the throne said, "I am making everything new!"*

Doesn't that last declaration by God describe what you have learned about yourself so far?

ACTIVATION 8-1

Please list in the blanks the names of people, whom you know personally, who are already manifesting these things with confidence. (Ignore the % blanks for now.)

____ % Spiritual Perception

_____

____ % Undeserving Beloved of God

_____

____ % Member of a New Race of Spirit-born men

_____

____ % Spirit-dominant, Spirit-sustained

_____

____ % Continual Rest & Communion with God

_____

____ % Fully Equipped Ruler with Will & Words

_____

Please note: maybe there were no names you could list. There might be a good reason we'll soon consider. Don't be discouraged!

ACTIVATION 8-2

In the ____ % above, put how much you think you get it. Use 0% if not at all (or totally disagree). Use 100% if you totally have been experiencing these things. And of course any percentage in-between.

ACTIVATION 8-3

In the diagram below, write the names of people that you personally know, according to your servanthood to them.

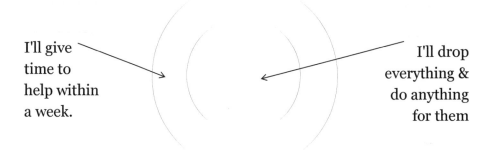

I'll give time to help within a week.

I'll drop everything & do anything for them

You are a Minister in the Church—Jesus' Eternal Bride. The Christians you just listed get to benefit from your ministry.

ACTIVATION 8-4

You are also a member of this Church. So let's look the other way. Activation four is a flip of #3. Write the names of people you personally know, according to their servanthood to you.

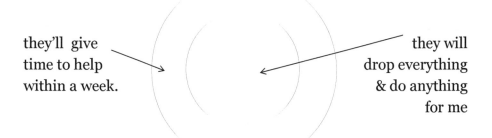

they'll give time to help within a week.

they will drop everything & do anything for me

Do you have no names for folks who will drop everything and do anything for you? Don't be disheartened or feel rejected. Keep reading.

The purpose of these is to take a snapshot of your fellowship circle. We have used Jesus' own tough standard to draw out those whom you love with His love, and vice versa. The larger group, those who will help you in a week, are important. The combined list are the people who manifest God's love for you. They have favor for you, and that comes from Him.

Reviewing your list, are there some Christians missing? Perhaps surprising omissions? There are many Christians with whom you share the emotions of love, affection, fondness and commonality. These can be mistaken for fellowship in the Spirit, of the Spirit-born. That's not to make light of them, but rather to illustrate who you really are. Removing the blindfold reveals that you are a Minister with authority in the Body of Christ to express His sacrificial love.

Consider a place where you gather with other people—a sporting event, a restaurant, or a voting place. We have a civilized society and 99% of the people there understand getting along, avoiding divisive issues, respecting each other. This is civil behavior. Like Frank Burns said in the 1970's series, M*A*S*H, "It's nice to be nice to the nice."

But this is not Christian love.

Consider church. Look at how nice 99% of the people are. A common identity unifies them, as members of that church.

But this is not Christian love. So what is? If you are an essential expression of God's love for His followers, how does that expression happen? Jesus answered that in John 13:13-17, after He washed the disciples' feet.

You call me 'Teacher' and 'Lord,' and rightly so, for that is what I am. Now that I, your Lord and Teacher, have washed your feet, you also should wash one another's feet. I have set you an example that you should do as I have done for you. I tell you the truth, no servant is greater than his master, nor is

a messenger greater than the one who sent him. Now that you
know these things, you will be blessed if you do them.

Washing feet was a servant's task. It permitted no pride of place. Jesus pointedly mentions His place with them—Lord, Teacher, master and sender. He surrendered all pride associated with these, to serve those He loved.

One of His motives is in the last verse: He wants you to be blessed. People sometimes feel obligated to serve another. Their personality or upbringing can compel them. And there are those who serve to get. But Jesus wants you to serve so that you can walk in the same blessing of God that He did.

In the last chapter on rulership, we saw Jesus' repeated and continual example and emphasis on servanthood. Let's consider it from a different angle. Did we learn that Christian fellowship was niceness, from Jesus? Did membership, getting along, looking good, or following social convention dominate His attention? How about Paul's? Peter's?

In fact, the one rebuke of an apostle recorded in the early church is when Peter did exactly those things. He substituted getting along, pleasing men and following the expectations of others for true Christian ministry. It's recorded in Galatians 2.

Jesus almost never—if at all—placed importance on pleasing men. As a dinner guest, for example in Luke 7:36-50, He was not dominated by custom and expectations. His time in the home of Simon the Pharisee appears to have begun with feelings of mutual respect, from 7:36. But when His presence there became known, a prostitute walks into the home of this religious leader. Now that's not a typical Sunday lunch after church, is it? Yet, Simon doesn't escort her out but instead permits her presence. So far, so good.

What finally breaks down Simon's civil tolerance of her presence? She wept on Jesus' feet, mixed her tears with her perfume, and wiped them with her hair. Simon interprets Jesus' acceptance of this sensual touching as proof that Jesus isn't a prophet. That is to say, Jesus isn't holy because He lets sinners touch him. Simon's disdain for her and for Jesus might have begun showing at that point.

Jesus goes on to commend the prostitute and highlight where her servanthood and faith exceeded those of his religious host.

What we mistake for love—time and activities together under our social conventions—is not the Bible meaning, as good as they are. This is just one example where we like Simon would consider this a terrible fellowship dinner. There are many others, James 2:1-13 being perhaps the most incisive.

So you are an essential expression of God's love for people and a minister in His eternal Bride the Church. What does that actually look like?

It looks like this: you serve as if Jesus is living in you. Which, how about that?! He is.

Servanthood is a frequent topic at Christian leadership training. If I have heard one sermon on servanthood I have heard hundreds. But here we are considering what you are, Christian, and what you are is an authorized servant. You have the permit to serve God in a matter of utmost priority to Him—His Bride, the Church.

Your blindfold is off, and you now see who you really are—a re-formed creature who is spiritually perceptive, an undeserving beneficiary of His love, someone in continual rest and communion with God, endowed with the created-in qualities we have considered. What's the most natural thing for you to do, if not express His love? It's not a moral issue or a religious issue. It is an issue of your intimacy with Him.

What God serves indicates what is valuable, important and essential to Him—and that is the people He puts in your path, to receive His love from you. You are serving God, joining with Him in loving His saints.

Jesus gave us this guidance, the only new commandment He gave, in John 13:34-35.

A new command I give you: Love one another. As I have loved you, so you must love one another. By this all men will know that you are my disciples, if you love one another.

You lay down your all for Him by laying down your all for your brother and your sister. When the Almighty Holy God of the entire universe washed the feet of those 12 men—including the one who would betray him—He unleashed a shock wave on the earth that has rippled to you. If you love Him, this is what you will do. Period.

What permission remains to you for pursuing your American dream? None. Not for the 1st century Roman dream or any alternative seduction this world offers. John understood this clearly when he wrote I John 3:16-18.

This is how we know what love is: Jesus Christ laid down his life for us. And we ought to lay down our lives for our brothers. If anyone has material possessions and sees his brother in need but has no pity on him, how can the love of God be in him? Dear children, let us not love with words or tongue but with actions and in truth.

That's why a Christian doesn't serve to get. A follower of Jesus serves naturally, as he walks in God's love and intimacy. And what an intimacy it is! Jesus describes it in John 15:9-15.

As the Father has loved me, so have I loved you. Now remain in my love. If you obey my commands, you will remain in my love, just as I have obeyed my Father's commands and remain in his love. I have told you this so that my joy may be in you and that your joy may be complete. My command is this: Love each other as I have loved you. Greater love has no one than this, that he lay down his life for his friends. You are my friends if you do what I command. I no longer call you servants, because a servant does not know his master's business. Instead, I have

called you friends, for everything that I learned from my
Father I have made known to you.

Jesus made you His follower. Included in that is far more than nice participation in happy fellowship activities, far more than information transfer, accurate beliefs, and compliant behavior. He says it twice: you get to remain in His love. He says you get to have an identical joy to His, and to have that joy in a complete way. And you are privy to His heart, and to His thoughts. He invites you to His intimate friendship when He says this.

Christian, what are you? You are someone with a new genetic makeup for pleasure. All your pleasure lights turn on when you share His love with Him for your your brother and sister.

Apostle Paul felt this way in I Corinthians 9:19, 22-23 & 27. All his sufferings are so he can share in the blessings of the gospel.

Though I am free and belong to no man, I make myself a slave
to everyone, to win as many as possible....I have become all
things to all men so that by all possible means I might save
some. I do all this for the sake of the gospel, that I may share
in its blessings. ...I beat my body and make it my slave so that
after I have preached to others, I myself will not be disqualified
for the prize.

Laying down your all for your brothers is Paul's theme in his letter to the Philippian assembly. He uses 5 examples there of servanthood to drive home one point, stated in 2:3-4.

Do nothing out of selfish ambition or vain conceit, but in
humility consider others better than yourselves. Each of you
should look not only to your own interests, but also to the
interests of others.

His first example is himself, in 1:21-25. Listen to the love he expresses on God's behalf when he resolves to live to minister, rather than to resign to death. Bear in mind he is in chains and under Roman guard when he writes this.

For to me, to live is Christ and to die is gain. If I am to go on living in the body, this will mean fruitful labor for me. Yet what shall I choose? I do not know! I am torn between the two: I desire to depart and be with Christ, which is better by far; but it is more necessary for you that I remain in the body. Convinced of this, I know that I will remain, and I will continue with all of you for your progress and joy in the faith.

Paul has to respond to some gospel preachers with base motives, and even there shows how He shares in God's joy. in Philippians 1:15-18.

It is true that some preach Christ out of envy and rivalry, but others out of goodwill. The latter do so in love, knowing that I am put here for the defense of the gospel. The former preach Christ out of selfish ambition, not sincerely, supposing that they can stir up trouble for me while I am in chains. But what does it matter? The important thing is that in every way, whether from false motives or true, Christ is preached. And because of this I rejoice.

Paul exemplifies a man who considers his expression of God's love for people to be essential. His second example in 2:5-7 is Jesus, obviously more essential.

Your attitude should be the same as that of Christ Jesus:

Who, being in very nature God,
    did not consider equality with God something to be

grasped,
but made himself nothing,
  taking the very nature of a servant,
  being made in human likeness.

Third is Timothy, and Paul's description of Timothy is striking, in Philippians 2:20-22.

I have no one else like him, who takes a genuine interest in your welfare. For everyone looks out for his own interests, not those of Jesus Christ. But you know that Timothy has proved himself, because as a son with his father he has served with me in the work of the gospel.

Doesn't that give you pause?

ACTIVATION 8-5

List the people whose name you can put in this blank: *I have no friend like* _____ *, who takes a genuine interest in your welfare.*

_____

_____

_____

List who would put your name there.

_____

_____

_____

Notice the apt description of people generally, and perhaps even the Christians around you: *everyone looks out for his own interest, not those of Jesus Christ.*

This is the measure that we saw Jesus use in deciding whether someone followed Him—they laid down their own interest and served His. Such a person will always be in the minority of a world against God. But is it not abundantly clear by now, that what you are, Christian, requires this laying down of your interests?

True fellowship occurs among such fellows—when one person lays down his or her interests. Bible study doesn't have to be present, nor does the action of Bible study indicate the presence of true biblical fellowship. Same with preaching, same with eating and pot lucks—nor any of our other shallow associations with "fellowship."

YOU are an essential expression of God's love. You are Spirit-born and He has made His home in you. Where less-aware Christians can be satisfied by customary group activities as fellowship, you no longer can. Your blindfold has fallen off. You can only be satisfied by being with Him—an intimacy of expressing your shared love for His people.

It may have already happened to you, the isolation of knowing God well, with spiritual perception being activated. Maybe there were no names you could list in activations one and four. Don't be discouraged. Maybe it is telling you that you are the one person in your circle of friends called Christian who is really after God. It's happened to more saints than you can imagine.

It's possible that you are the one who is most spiritually perceptive. And it's also possible that they may not follow Jesus to His satisfaction, and therefore do not relate to you.

Expressing God's love, enjoying His completed joy, remaining in His love yourself—these can occur with just one saint with God living in him. There in that one person, you, is the fellowship of two wills, yours the inferior and His the superior.

What did Jesus mean when He said, *Remain in His love*? You find that His will is ravished with passion for His Bride, the Church. When His will within you is over your own, you gain the same ravished passion.

It's no accident that He reveals the Church to be His Bride in Ephesians 5:25-33. That's where Apostle Paul tells how a man shows love to his wife. He equates Christ's love for the Church to a man's passion for the care of his own self. That's ravished! Song of Solomon makes this plain, and doubtless influenced Paul's understanding of the Church. It is a racy book of steamy passion between a husband and wife. Not only is God's superior love in full view, but also the various responses of the Church in the process of yielding to His passion for us.

As your awareness of God within you grows and deepens, no loneliness, no shyness, no fear of people in all the world can keep you from serving other Christians with His love. His passion compels you. You are essential to them. You are essential to His Bride, the whole Church. Through you, and only through you, and uniquely through you, He is able to express His love for others as He can through no one else. And this can be said of everyone who follows Jesus.

And when you serve other Christians, poof! There's the fellowship that satisfies you.

Paul's 4th example is Epaphroditus (e-PAF-ro-DI-tus) in Philippians 2:26, 28.

> But I think it is necessary to send back to you Epaphroditus, my brother, fellow worker and fellow soldier, who is also your messenger, whom you sent to take care of my needs. For he longs for all of you and is distressed because you heard he was ill. He almost died for the work of Christ, risking his life to make up for the help you could not give me.

You just read a description of someone who has laid down their interests, to express the love of God and to minister to someone in His Church. He cares more for their worry than for himself.

The 5th example Paul gives to the Philippian church is their own church. Consider 1:4-5, 3:25, & 4:10,14-16,18.

> In all my prayers for all of you, I always pray with joy because of your partnership in the gospel from the first day until now...

...Epaphroditus, my brother, fellow worker and fellow soldier, who is also your messenger, whom you sent to take care of my needs.

I rejoice greatly in the Lord that at last you have renewed your concern for me. Indeed, you have been concerned, but you had no opportunity to show it ...Yet it was good of you to share in my troubles. Moreover, as you Philippians know, in the early days of your acquaintance with the gospel, when I set out from Macedonia, not one church shared with me in the matter of giving and receiving, except you only; for even when I was in Thessalonica, you sent me aid again and again when I was in need. ...I have received full payment and even more; I am amply supplied, now that I have received from Epaphroditus the gifts you sent.

Wow, how they laid down their interests to serve Jesus' interest in advancing Paul's ministry. And Paul didn't even attend their church. Amazingly, when he started it in Acts 16, he was there physically only a matter of days before the uproar that led to his expulsion from Philippi. Yet here they are, sending people and money to serve Apostle Paul, even in an era of much greater insecurity of travel and healthcare (compared to ours).

While Paul is known as the apostle to the Gentiles, it may also be accurate to call him the apostle of the Church. The Holy Spirit revealed to Apostle Paul what God was doing in this Church of His. Jesus only used the word "church" two times prior to His ascension. That's striking, isn't it? He said virtually nothing about church. And the word isn't used in Acts until long after Pentecost, in 5:11. Yet today when we think of Christianity, we think church. (How did that happen? For in-depth understanding of this, I highly recommend the book *The Eternal Church* by Bishop Bill Hamon of Christian International.)

But our interest here is to place you, a Spirit-born ruler who has spiritual perception, in His Church, and for what reasons? You are an essential expression of His love for them. You are a minister to them. Yes, this is a remarkably simple understanding of you. Paul received this from the Holy Spirit, and wrote it in Ephesians 4:7-8.

> But to each one of us grace has been given as Christ apportioned it. This is why it says: "When he ascended on high, he led captives in his train and gave gifts to men."

He then describes the five leadership gifts that Jesus gave His Church in 4:11.

> It was he who gave some to be apostles, some to be prophets, some to be evangelists, and some to be pastors and teachers,

Paul gives two other lists of gifts from God in Romans 12:6b-8 and I Corinthians 12:8-10.

> If a man's gift is prophesying, let him use it in proportion to his faith. If it is serving, let him serve; if it is teaching, let him teach; if it is encouraging, let him encourage; if it is contributing to the needs of others, let him give generously; if it is leadership, let him govern diligently; if it is showing mercy, let him do it cheerfully.
>
> To one there is given through the Spirit the message of wisdom, to another the message of knowledge by means of the same Spirit, to another faith by the same Spirit, to another gifts of healing by that one Spirit, to another miraculous powers, to another prophecy, to another distinguishing between spirits, to another speaking in different kinds of tongues, and to still another the interpretation of tongues.

God says your ministry is important. He gives it to you. Your gifts are given, to help you share with Him in loving His people, His Bride. Paul says this before each gift list, in Romans 12:4-6a and I Corinthians 12:4-7.

Just as each of us has one body with many members, and these members do not all have the same function, so in Christ we who are many form one body, and each member belongs to all the others. We have different gifts, according to the grace given us.

There are different kinds of gifts, but the same Spirit. There are different kinds of service, but the same Lord. There are different kinds of working, but the same God works all of them in all men. Now to each one the manifestation of the Spirit is given for the common good.

And likewise, God affirms our one race, our one identity. Here's what Paul writes in Romans 12:10,16 and I Corinthians 12:3,18,24-25,27.

Be devoted to one another in brotherly love. Honor one another above yourselves...Live in harmony with one another. Do not be proud, but be willing to associate with people of low position.

For we were all baptized by one Spirit into one body— whether Jews or Greeks, slave or free —and we were all given the one Spirit to drink....But in fact God has arranged the parts in the body, every one of them, just as he wanted them to be. ...But God has combined the members of the body and has given greater honor to the parts that lacked it, so that there should be no division in the body, but that its parts should have equal concern for each other...Now you are the body of Christ, and each one of you is a part of it.

Paul expressed the same revelation from God, that we are one identity, one race, one unified being, in Ephesians 4:4-6.

There is one body and one Spirit —just as you were called to one hope when you were called — one Lord, one faith, one baptism; one God and Father of all, who is over all and through all and in all.

It is this body of Christ in which you are an essential part, an expression of God's love, a minister. Why did Jesus give the five leadership gifts we saw above? Paul says in Ephesians 4:12, for you, minister Christian.

> *to prepare God's people for works of service, so that the body of Christ may be built up.*

Notice your ministry: "works of service." God has provided that your works of service are an essential ingredient of building up His Bride. That is quite an honor. It's like being asked to be a lady-in-waiting of a mighty princess on the day of her marriage to the King Himself. You do all in your power to tend her dress, perfect her hair, adorn her appearance, and maintain her attention to her Lover. No attention to yourself is necessary or beneficial, for all the satisfaction you could possibly need is provided by participating in this consummation of intimacy.

ACTIVATION 8-6

Let's benchmark with an activation. Write down in the blanks below what specific servanthood actions you have heard taught and encouraged.

_____

_____

_____

Now write down what servanthood actions you feel you do well, in a church setting.

_____

_____

_____

These will serve well as we consider the water in which your thinking is swimming. This helped us in previous chapters. Understanding that we are Spirit-dominant and Spirit-sustained requires us to identify the poisonous thinking of materialism and naturalism. Enjoying our continual rest and communion with God got a boost from naming and maiming the wrongheadedness of transactional thinking about God.

Now let's not throw out the baby with the bathwater. These errors in thinking and seeing could only have developed in an environment and society with a biblical underpinning. A transactional understanding of relating to God is a shallow mutation of a foundational Christian truth: a person can have a relationship with God. Both materialism and naturalism are simply hollow God-emptied distortions of a foundational Christian truth: all that God made is good.

Likewise with our society's individualism. It could only have developed because the Bible said that God cares for people as individuals and commits to covenants with individuals. Think about that. It's incredible. No non-biblical religion has that concept nor would dare to propose it.

That's the baby—that the individual matters. The dirty bathwater to throw out is this: that the individual matters most. And its impact on your satisfaction of expressing God's love is not good. Combined with materialism, individualism prompts us to identify servanthood primarily as helping with the world's goods and arrangements. The backwards effect of this is to subject Christian servanthood to the standards of this world which is under the control of the evil one.

Individualism also introduces a self-focus to our servanthood, so that we are the issue in our servanthood. "Did I serve well enough? Was it pleasing to them? Will they ask me again?" Selfish servanthood can be manipulative or using. Selfishness can make servanthood condescending also: "My agenda is more important so I will squeeze my brother's need into my agenda if I can."

Let's focus now on just two New Testament patterns of sharing in God's love for His people.

The first pattern is tithing and giving. It's a subject that Christians are either passionate about or afraid of. But let's look at the water our thinking swims in. Individualism makes tithing about me. So how many Christians individualistically think that tithing is a way to get God to bless them? How much Christian teaching advocates tithing as the path to riches?

Individualism leads Christians to be takers rather than givers. This attitude plagues our nation today. Yet the entire fellowship of Christ's Body is to minister to one another—not suck ministry from one another.

Again Paul praises the example of the Philippian Christians when he cites their attitude to the Corinthians, in II Corinthians 8:1-5. (Philippi is in Macedonia.)

> *And now, brothers, we want you to know about the grace that God has given the Macedonian churches. Out of the most severe trial, their overflowing joy and their extreme poverty welled up in rich generosity. For I testify that they gave as much as they were able, and even beyond their ability. Entirely on their own, they urgently pleaded with us for the privilege of sharing in this service to the saints. And they did not do as we expected, but they gave themselves first to the Lord and then to us in keeping with God's will.*

They exemplify Jesus' own example, Paul says in II Corinthians 8:9.

> *For you know the grace of our Lord Jesus Christ, that though he was rich, yet for your sakes he became poor, so that you through his poverty might become rich.*

Paul makes it clear in 9:7-11 that we are a fellowship of givers.

Each man should give what he has decided in his heart to give, not reluctantly or under compulsion, for God loves a cheerful giver. And God is able to make all grace abound to you, so that in all things at all times, having all that you need, you will abound in every good work. As it is written:

"He has scattered abroad his gifts to the poor; his righteousness endures forever."

Now he who supplies seed to the sower and bread for food will also supply and increase your store of seed and will enlarge the harvest of your righteousness. You will be made rich in every way so that you can be generous on every occasion, and through us your generosity will result in thanksgiving to God.

We are a fellowship of givers because God is a giver. It comes out of our sharing His love for His people. Apostle John had a plainspoken way of putting it in I John 3:16-17.

This is how we know what love is: Jesus Christ laid down his life for us. And we ought to lay down our lives for our brothers. If anyone has material possessions and sees his brother in need but has no pity on him, how can the love of God be in him?

Laying down our lives is Jesus' definition of His followers, and we lay down our lives for each other. We look after each others' interests.

David also saw the deception of withholding from God. He pronounced the truth in an assembly of all Israel in I Chronicles 29:14-18.

But who am I, and who are my people, that we should be able to give as generously as this? Everything comes from you, and we have given you only what comes from your hand. We are aliens and strangers in your sight, as were all our forefathers. Our days on earth are like a shadow, without hope. O Lord our God, as for all this abundance that we have provided for building you a temple for your Holy Name, it comes from your hand, and all of it belongs to you. I know, my God, that you test the heart and are pleased with integrity. All these things have I given willingly and with honest intent. And now I have seen with joy how willingly your people who are here have given to you.

The individualist in us looks at tithing and says, "What do I get out of it?" Some get recognition as in Matthew 6:1. Others get manipulation and leverage as Obadiah exhibited in I Kings 18:9-14. Another self-centered motive for servanthood is commerce, as Jesus points out in Luke 6:33-35. Much teaching promotes tithing as a way to get more from God, and where's the love in that?

But those are not you. You are an essential expression of God's love to His Bride, and you minister in it. It pushes your pleasure buttons to express that love to those He loves.

A second New Testament pattern of showing Jesus' love is ministering vigilance and fidelity to our faith. As a minister of Jesus in His Body, a minister of the unseen which is eternal (II Corinthians 4:18), you can keep the truth in front of your brothers, and encourage them in living holy lives.

We saw that God commanded this mutual care and vigilance in Deuteronomy 6:6-9.

These commandments that I give you today are to be upon your hearts. Impress them on your children. Talk about them when you sit at home and when you walk along the road, when you lie down and when you get up. Tie them as symbols on your hands and bind them on your foreheads. Write them on the door frames of your houses and on your gates.

As a result, teaching and correction receive emphasis in the Bible. Think of it: God is willing to make a covenant with an individual person. God elevates the individual person as a free moral agent able to covenant with Him. We share His love for our brothers and sisters by keeping God's truths before their eyes.

The apostles took this ministry of truth-reminding very seriously and so must we. Even if the apostles seemed to be restating themselves, they did so anyway, like a parent to a teenager. Listen to their servant heart wanting us to remember, their vigilant attention that no one forget, their passion to keep before us the unseen real.

Then they returned to Lystra, Iconium and Antioch, strengthening the disciples and encouraging them to remain true to the faith. "We must go through many hardships to enter the kingdom of God," they said. (Paul & Barnabas in Acts 14:21-22, revisiting churches they had established)

So be on your guard! Remember that for three years I never stopped warning each of you night and day with tears. (Paul to Ephesian elders in Acts 20:31)

It is no trouble for me to write the same things to you again, and it is a safeguard for you. ..For, as I have often told you before and now say again even with tears, many live as enemies of the cross of Christ. (Paul to the Philippian assembly in Philippians 3:1, 18)

Finally, brothers, we instructed you how to live in order to please God, as in fact you are living. Now we ask you and urge you in the Lord Jesus to do this more and more. For you know what instructions we gave you by the authority of the Lord Jesus....Don't you remember that when I was with you I used to tell you these things?...So then, brothers, stand firm and hold to the teachings we passed on to you, whether by word of mouth or by letter. (Paul to the Thessalonians, in I Thessalonians 4:1-2, II Thessalonians 2:5,15)

Apostle Peter had the same heart as Paul to keep the truth ever before the Church.

I have written to you briefly, encouraging you and testifying that this is the true grace of God. Stand fast in it. (I Peter 5:12)

So I will always remind you of these things, even though you know them and are firmly established in the truth you now have. I think it is right to refresh your memory as long as I live in the tent of this body….And I will make every effort to see that after my departure you will always be able to remember these things. (II Peter 1:12-13,15)

Dear friends, this is now my second letter to you. I have written both of them as reminders to stimulate you to wholesome thinking. I want you to recall the words spoken in the past by the holy prophets and the command given by our Lord and Savior through your apostles. (II Peter 3:1-2)

This apostolic priority upon continual reminders translates poorly into our society. Our conditioning is to view repetition as boring. Perhaps seeing the same TV show over and over is boring, or repetitive work on an assembly line—but to paint the truth from God's heart as boring, ever, in any way, is an enemy trick. This trick makes the teachers and preachers in our midst seem like old hat, antiquated, out of touch, when they repeatedly—like the apostles— hold the same truths in front of us over and over.

And this blindfold of boringness shames Christians into not bringing these important divine truths up with friends. Yet this is exactly what Jesus-followers are to do. Consider the admonitions we are given, to exercise our responsibility of vigilance for each other, in Hebrews.

See to it, brothers, that none of you has a sinful, unbelieving heart that turns away from the living God. But encourage one another daily, as long as it is called Today, so that none of you may be hardened by sin's deceitfulness. (3:12-13)

Let us, therefore, make every effort to enter that rest, so that no one will fall by following their example of disobedience. (4:11)

And let us consider how we may spur one another on toward love and good deeds. Let us not give up meeting together, as some are in the habit of doing, but let us encourage one another. (10:24-25)

See to it that no one misses the grace of God and that no bitter root grows up to cause trouble and defile many. See that no one is sexually immoral, or is godless like Esau...(12:15-16)

See to it that you do not refuse him who speaks. (12:25)

"See to it"—a compelling refrain describing what a Spirit-born, spiritually perceptive person does for his brothers and sisters in their new race. And this is addressed to all the Body, not merely the leaders. Hebrews 13:17 makes it plain that the "See to it" admonitions are not just the leaders' responsibility but everyone's, and that as a Body there is accountability for each of us to help each other.

Sometimes Christians fail to "see to it" because they don't know how. There may be a fear of causing trouble. Each church has an established protocol for helping fellow members when a "See to it" is needed. Hebrews 13:17 tells us to submit to that protocol established by our church authority. "See to it" service does not only mean directly. In a church setting in fact, the pastor, board or other leadership has set a process that you can cooperate with in discharging your responsibility to the brethren.

You are an essential expression of God's love. This love manifests when someone is protected from sin. Consider James 5:16.

Therefore confess your sins to each other and pray for each other so that you may be healed.

Apostle John charges each of us with the vigilance for one another in I John 5:16.

If anyone sees his brother commit a sin that does not lead to death, he should pray and God will give him life.

Paul gives you the same ministry in Galatians 6:1-2.

Brothers, if someone is caught in a sin, you who are spiritual should restore him gently. But watch yourself, or you also may be tempted. Carry each other's burdens, and in this way you will fulfill the law of Christ.

You are a minister in Christ's Eternal bride, the Church, and duly authorized to "See to it" by working with its leaders. In fact, you are accountable to do so.

ACTIVATION 8-7

Look back at the names you listed in activations one and four. Is there an overlap, some names on both lists? If so, write those in the leftmost blanks only, the names on both Activations one and four. NAMES ON BOTH

_____   _____   _____

_____   _____   _____

_____   _____   _____

ACTIVATION 8-8

Get the phone numbers and the emails for those folks and write them in the other two blanks by their names.

ACTIVATION 8-9

Before you start reading chapter 9, call two of the above and after a chat, ask them if there is anything you can do for them.

After doing this two times, I am certain you will be addicted to the pleasure shared with God who has ordained you a minister in His Body, the Church.

If there are no names common to list one and four, or perhaps even empty blanks, you can consider that you may be the farthest along among your fellowship. As long as you are in that fellowship circle, you are duly authorized to serve in the ways we've talked about. Ask Him to reveal to you His heart for them. Enter into your Father's love for them. Intercede for what matters to them. Minister to your brothers and sisters. Find the ones who want to be like you and serve them.

It's possible you need to widen your circle of brothers and sisters. For example, I do not go to church with my closest friends. We meet for lunch and pray afterwards during the week. Every geographical area has people who want to be sold out for Jesus, if they could only meet someone like you, who is like what you have been reading. You are the magnet, and the Holy Spirit nature within you.

Whomever you are with, serve and minister to them. That's how to enjoy your intimacy with God. Walk with Him in love, and all your pleasures will be satisfied.

God, I deeply enjoy sharing Your love for Your Bride.
Thank you for sharing it with me.
I yield to even more than ever!

CHAPTER 9:
YOU & YOUR RACE ARE A SIGN & A FIRST EVIDENCE OF THE COMING AGE, A CONVICTING INFLUENCE TO THOSE AROUND YOU, PREPARING THE WAY FOR GOD TO REVEAL HIMSELF TO THEM

As we've seen, with God living in you as His home on earth, nothing is the same. A new normal is in effect and it takes some getting used to. So with our first benchmarking activation, the topic is your interactions with people who don't follow Jesus. Warning: this may be challenging to your definition of "love."

ACTIVATION 9-1

Please list the places—such as "work," "Neighborhood," "softball"—where you have the most interaction with unbelievers and people who don't evidence love for Jesus.

1. _____

2. _____

3. _____

4. _____

Now for each of those places or groups, list some people's names—regardless of how well you know them.

Names for place 1. _____

_____

Names for place 2. _____

_____

Names for place 3. _____

_____

Names for place 4.   _____

_____

On the above list, cross out the ones who think of themselves as Christian, but whose life says otherwise. Like this: ~~name~~.

ACTIVATION 9-2

This time, list people that you know personally. On the right side of the scale below, put the names of those whom you feel are really following Jesus. On the left, write the names of those who think they are Christians but you feel they are not following Jesus as we saw earlier in this book.

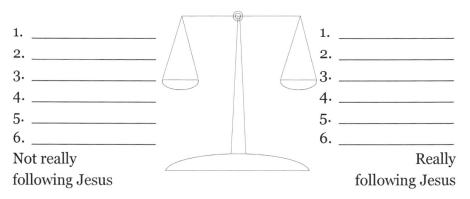

1. _____   1. _____
2. _____   2. _____
3. _____   3. _____
4. _____   4. _____
5. _____   5. _____
6. _____   6. _____

Not really   Really
following Jesus   following Jesus

ACTIVATION 9-3

On the scale below, put an X to show how judgmental you felt doing the above.

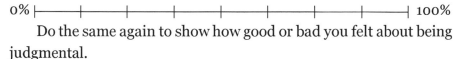

0% ⊢———+———+———+———+———+———+———⊣ 100%

Do the same again to show how good or bad you felt about being judgmental.

0% ⊢———+———+———+———+———+———+———⊣ 100%

The purpose of these activations was to reveal our social training not to judge others. "Ye shall not judge" is now modern America's greatest commandment—and a blindfold soon to be removed.

Our goal in this chapter is for you to receive the Scripture's teaching that you are a walking, talking zone of conviction and attraction to those who are not saved. You are a carrier of God's conviction to the people He sends. To be effective you have to think biblically about judging. Yes, some people will respond as if you are an unwelcome presence.

But not everyone. To some people you are also a carrier of God's attraction. The Holy Spirit is wooing them with His awesome presence, which has just come near to them on your two legs.

Conviction is a customary Christian word. Attraction results because of the desirability of what the Holy Spirit wants to achieve—people to know God, and God to live in them as He does in us. His invigorating love is affecting people, from His mini-headquarters in you.

Poverty of spirit, mourning, meekness and hunger can only arise when we are convicted. And into the vacuum of our vanishing self-reliance floods the power and love of the most wonderful Father.

Our gospel is about God's Father-love being enjoyed by people. Our gospel says that people are not right with God, cannot enjoy that Father-love and can do nothing to solve it. Instead, God has solved it once for all for everyone who yields to His Father-love by following Jesus as Lord and Savior.

Yes, in His infinite love He wanted to restore our fellowship with Him. In Isaiah 57:15, He tells who He seeks.

Build up, build up, prepare the road!
  Remove the obstacles out of the way of my people."
For this is what the high and lofty One says—
  he who lives forever, whose name is holy:
"I live in a high and holy place,
  but also with him who is contrite and lowly in spirit,
to revive the spirit of the lowly
  and to revive the heart of the contrite.
I will not accuse forever,

> nor will I always be angry,
> for then the spirit of man would grow faint before me—
>   the breath of man that I have created.
> I was enraged by his sinful greed;
>   I punished him, and hid my face in anger,
>   yet he kept on in his willful ways.
> I have seen his ways, but I will heal him;
>   I will guide him and restore comfort to him,
>   creating praise on the lips of the mourners in Israel.
> Peace, peace, to those far and near,"
>   says the LORD. "And I will heal them."

Who wouldn't want to be the recipient of this holy love? Who wouldn't gladly be lowly in spirit, if God living in you is the result? What sane person would refuse to be contrite when that's what opens the door to all God's peace and healing and comfort?

People in our society have been accustomed to think of God transactionally as we have discussed. That presumes that we have something to offer Him in a transaction.

But in the passage above, the only way to receive from God is a lowly spirit and contrite heart. How do you get these? When your offensive ways are revealed to you—when you see you cannot make up for or paper over them.

So it is with every person God sends to you. One of the most loving things you can do is help people see their situation, and become lowly of spirit and contrite of heart.

But are you more sold on not judging, than on carrying His conviction and attraction? Than on living among the people of the world as a new creation in a new race? If your answer has been "yes, more sold on not judging," then your perception of people's spiritual situation has been disarmed. A commitment not to judge disarms your spiritual effectiveness. It makes you partner to their destruction.

Not judging seems loving but actually is not compassionate at all.

We must confess the American non-judging water that our thinking is swimming in. Our thinking requires correction. We repent for yielding to its pre-eminence over biblical values. I repent for remaining silent when wrong went excused. Let's repent that we allow sin that damns to be called okay.

We, the Church, are waking up, and it's great. But we are way behind the growth curve in this area. We lack competency for judging with love. We haven't developed our wisdom for simultaneously convicting and attracting. As a result of our immaturity in this as a Church in America, our responses have been all over the place.

On the one hand, major denominations have re-interpreted the Bible rather than offend those who practice profligacy, licentiousness, greed, homosexuality, cowardice. On the other hand are churches and Christian groups who harshly reject those who haven't repented. They erect such barriers to God's saving love that they lend credence to the derogatory term, "Bible-thumpers." Even in writing this chapter, I am concerned that our group immaturity in this area will lead some to become harshly judgmental.

Yet between these extremes it is possible to be Christlike in judging with love being felt. It is possible to convict and attract simultaneously. It is possible for a church body to have restorative disciplinary procedures and trained leaders charged with a loving vigilance for the church. It is possible to love the sinner, to put up no walls, to overcome evil with love, and also to judge the sin that costs the sinner so dearly.

Yes, it takes maturity. So let's get that maturity going and not be passive about it. The lost need us to see who we are and stop tolerating blindfolds. Yes, there will be messes, Hebrews 5:14 suggests. It says we train our senses to discern good and evil by constant use. In other words—trial and error is the process.

What is judging, in the Bible, and why is it loving? Jesus himself gave us what American society distorted to its greatest commandment, in Matthew 7:1-2.

Do not judge, or you too will be judged. For in the same way you judge others, you will be judged, and with the measure you use, it will be measured to you.

Let's see if Jesus practiced what we think He preached. His very next statements show how shallow our understanding of judging has been.

Do not give dogs what is sacred; do not throw your pearls to pigs. If you do, they may trample them under their feet, and then turn and tear you to pieces.

 Watch out for false prophets. They come to you in sheep's clothing, but inwardly they are ferocious wolves. By their fruit you will recognize them. Do people pick grapes from thorn bushes, or figs from thistles? Likewise every good tree bears good fruit, but a bad tree bears bad fruit. A good tree cannot bear bad fruit, and a bad tree cannot bear good fruit. Every tree that does not bear good fruit is cut down and thrown into the fire. Thus, by their fruit you will recognize them.

 Not everyone who says to me, 'Lord, Lord,' will enter the kingdom of heaven, but only he who does the will of my Father who is in heaven. Many will say to me on that day, 'Lord, Lord, did we not prophesy in your name, and in your name drive out demons and perform many miracles?' Then I will tell them plainly, 'I never knew you. Away from me, you evildoers!' (Matthew 7:6,15-20,21-23)

Can you imagine yourself saying something like this next one in a crowd?

Knowing their thoughts, Jesus said, "Why do you entertain evil thoughts in your hearts?

Then Jesus began to denounce the cities in which most of his miracles had been performed, because they did not repent. "Woe to you, Korazin! Woe to you, Bethsaida!

You brood of vipers, how can you who are evil say anything good? For out of the overflow of the heart the mouth speaks.

The knowledge of the secrets of the kingdom of heaven has been given to you, but not to them. (Matthew 9:4, 11:20, 12:34, 13:11)

This is just a short list, from 6 of Matthew's 28 chapters, that show Jesus clearly didn't think of judging the same way we do. He didn't think of His injunction, "Judge not lest you be judged," in the same way we do.

In fact, Jesus' judging gets worse—speaking from the American perspective, that is. Look at John's eyewitness record of how Jesus talked, from John 3:5, 4:16-18, and 5:37-38,42.

Jesus answered, "I tell you the truth, no one can enter the kingdom of God unless he is born of water and the Spirit."

He told her, "Go, call your husband and come back." "I have no husband," she replied. Jesus said to her, "You are right when you say you have no husband. The fact is, you have had five husbands, and the man you now have is not your husband. What you have just said is quite true."

You have never heard his [The Father's] voice nor seen his form, nor does his word dwell in you, for you do not believe the one he sent. You diligently study the Scriptures because you think that by them you possess eternal life. These are the Scriptures that testify about me, yet you refuse to come to me to have life. I do not accept praise from men, but I know you. I know that you do not have the love of God in your hearts.

Then there's what we might call the ultimate judgmentalism in John 8:44-47.

> *Jesus said to them, "If God were your Father, you would love me, for I came from God and now am here. I have not come on my own; but he sent me. Why is my language not clear to you? Because you are unable to hear what I say. You belong to your father, the devil, and you want to carry out your father's desire....The reason you do not hear is that you do not belong to God."*

You've just seen how "judgmental" Jesus was. How does our society tell us to respond to judgmental people and people who say things like that?

_____

_____

_____

Lest you think Jesus gets a pass because He really will be the Judge on Judgment Day, it's clear His NT apostles continued and advocated the habit. We'll continue with Peter, in Acts 5:3-4, 8:20-23 and II Peter 2:12,17. But please remember, soon we will see the love behind these. Hang on!

> *Then Peter said, "Ananias, how is it that Satan has so filled your heart that you have lied to the Holy Spirit...? You have not lied to men but to God."*
> *Peter answered: "May your money perish with you, because you thought you could buy the gift of God with money! You have no part or share in this ministry, because your heart is not right before God. Repent of this wickedness and pray to the Lord. Perhaps he will forgive you for having such a thought in your heart. For I see that you are full of bitterness and captive to sin."*

But these men blaspheme in matters they do not understand. They are like brute beasts, creatures of instinct, born only to be caught and destroyed, and like beasts they too will perish....These men are springs without water and mists driven by a storm. Blackest darkness is reserved for them.

John placed the same importance on identifying people's spiritual situation and responding properly, in I John 1:6, 2:4, 3:8 and II John 10-11.

If we claim to have fellowship with him yet walk in the darkness, we lie and do not live by the truth....The man who says, "I know him," but does not do what he commands is a liar, and the truth is not in him....He who does what is sinful is of the devil, because the devil has been sinning from the beginning.... If anyone comes to you and does not bring this teaching, do not take him into your house or welcome him. Anyone who welcomes him shares in his wicked work.

Jude echoes this in Jude 12-13--

These men are blemishes at your love feasts, eating with you without the slightest qualm—shepherds who feed only themselves. They are clouds without rain, blown along by the wind; autumn trees, without fruit and uprooted —twice dead. They are wild waves of the sea, foaming up their shame; wandering stars, for whom blackest darkness has been reserved forever.

What Apostle Paul says in I Corinthians 5:2,5,11-12 is very offensive to our ears.

Shouldn't you rather have been filled with grief and have put out of your fellowship the man who did this?...hand this man

over to Satan, so that the sinful nature may be destroyed and
his spirit saved on the day of the Lord.... now I am writing
you that you must not associate with anyone who calls himself
a brother but is sexually immoral or greedy, an idolater or a
slanderer, a drunkard or a swindler. With such a man do not
even eat. What business is it of mine to judge those outside the
church? Are you not to judge those inside?

Notice that Paul doesn't leave us the excuse of not being apostles. The Bible instructs that Christians and the Church must judge its members. There are many Scriptures in the New Testament that teach this.

Why is it necessary for a follower of Jesus to be judging? Because otherwise, you cannot prepare people to receive His self-revealing. Why do you think He wants more and more headquarters on earth? To reveal Himself to people, that they might repent and gain what you have—God within you. With every new believer, there is another God-in-a-person spreading conviction and attraction among those who are not saved. The American commandment "You shall not judge" short-circuits this most necessary ministry—it makes Christians embarrassed to wake people up to the sin that alienates God from them.

If the negative form of America's greatest commandment is "Do not judge," what are the positive forms? "Go along to get along." "Live and let live." "It's none of my business." And "be nice," which Frank Burns has been previously described saying in the TV series M.A.S.H., "It's nice to be nice to the nice."

Sure, be nice—but not at cost of obscuring God's judgment on sin and those who prefer it to Him. Not at the expense of disobeying what God says out of His Father-love for people.

Niceness and getting along are gross distortions of the love of God. These mutations, far removed from their origin in true Biblical love, are in your head as a result of long socialization. They serve one purpose: to shut you up so you can't help people confess and repent of their barriers against God. These distorted love-commands disarm you from your evangelistic role: to prepare the way for God to reveal Himself to the people you encounter.

In American society today, all encouragements to repentance are labeled as judgmentalism and intolerance. Encouraging someone to stop a behavior and repent is a big social no-no. It is people's quick choice to be offended that you would even describe something they do as sinful. Despite their choice, the offensiveness is blamed on you.

This pressure not to offend can force you into an argument with your own Creator. God arranged that only the poor in spirit, the mourning, the meek and the hungry are the blessed ones. He said repentance of sin is the only way to become that blessed. To gloss over or ridicule the necessity to repent for sin puts someone at argument with God's own arrangement.

This argument with God is a devilish lie that has infected American Christians. This is the lie that offending people is worse than offending God. Get rid of it—and fast. You become willfully blind to their pending damnation. It makes you the enemy of people's salvation. And it muzzles the carrier of conviction and attraction—namely, you.

That is definitely not something you want happening in your life. If you have been infected with this lie, the one hurt most by the muzzling may even be you yourself. Your devilish training not to judge applies to yourself, too. So you are locked out of identifying your own sins, out of confessing and repenting of it, and out of your own most blessed poverty of spirit.

Make no mistake about this: True Christian love encourages repentance and poverty of spirit. True Christian love does not make light of sin. True Christian love is restorative, not condemning.

Because of this, the *how* is as important as the *what*. That's clear in Galatians 6:1, II Corinthians 2:6-11, James 5:15-16, and I John 5:16.

Brothers, if someone is caught in a sin, you who are spiritual should restore him gently. But watch yourself, or you also may be tempted.

The punishment inflicted on him by the majority is sufficient for him. Now instead, you ought to forgive and comfort him, so that he will not be overwhelmed by excessive sorrow. I urge you, therefore, to reaffirm your love for him. The reason I wrote you was to see if you would stand the test and be obedient in everything. If you forgive anyone, I also forgive him. And what I have forgiven—if there was anything to forgive—I have forgiven in the sight of Christ for your sake, in order that Satan might not outwit us. For we are not unaware of his schemes.

And the prayer offered in faith will make the sick person well; the Lord will raise him up. If he has sinned, he will be forgiven. Therefore confess your sins to each other and pray for each other so that you may be healed. The prayer of a righteous man is powerful and effective.

If anyone sees his brother commit a sin that does not lead to death, he should pray and God will give him life.

The love of the brothers is clearly the manner as well as the motivating power in our judging. As stated earlier, the manner among believers is following the protocol established by the church leadership.

If this seems contradictory to your idea of Christianity, ask yourself these questions. Was Jesus loving? Or not? Were the NT authors loving? Or not? Yes, of course. Then there must be a way to love people with words they feel are judging, to help them see their need for Jesus.

The Apostle Paul clearly saw this as he wrote the Ephesians in 4:15-16. Love for Jesus and desire to be like Him and mature in Him is the motive, and love is the manner.

speaking the truth in love, we will in all things grow up into him who is the Head, that is, Christ. From him the whole body, joined and held together by every supporting ligament, grows and builds itself up in love, as each part does its work.

Speaking the truth in love is a maturing process. As we go through various circumstances we wrestle with what God's love wants done through us. As stated, we are way behind the curve of maturity on this. With your American tolerance-at-any-cost training, can you imagine yourself saying things like these that Jesus did in Matthew 23:15,27, and 33?

you make him twice as much a son of hell as you are.

You are like whitewashed tombs, which look beautiful on the outside but on the inside are full of dead men's bones and everything unclean. In the same way, on the outside you appear to people as righteous but on the inside you are full of hypocrisy and wickedness.

You snakes! You brood of vipers! How will you escape being condemned to hell?

How can it possibly be loving to talk like this? It's loving because everyone who doesn't follow Jesus lives in a fog—a fog that keeps them from seeing their danger of eternal punishment. It's loving because the enemy of every human continually maintains this fog. A society that cooperates with this deception is keeping people from being saved.

Listen to Paul's descriptions of this fog-penetrating love in II Corinthians 4:4 and Ephesians 5:8,11,13.

The god of this age has blinded the minds of unbelievers, so that they cannot see the light of the gospel of the glory of Christ, who is the image of God. For we do not preach ourselves, but Jesus Christ as Lord, and ourselves as your servants for Jesus' sake.

For you were once darkness, but now you are light in the Lord...Have nothing to do with the fruitless deeds of darkness, but rather expose them...But everything exposed by the light becomes visible, for it is light that makes everything visible.

Living this way is what is meant when Paul tells us to fit our feet *with the readiness that comes from the gospel of peace* (Ephesians 6:15). It is a readiness to speak truth about barriers and God's solution to the person He brings you. God Almighty arranged earth and time for you to encounter the person standing near you, because He wants peace with that person. He has ordained that in you He has someone to further prepare the way for God to reveal Himself to them. Yes, that's right, in you. That is what you are, Christian! Here's what God says in II Corinthians 5:19-20.

And he has committed to us the message of reconciliation. We are therefore Christ's ambassadors, as though God were making his appeal through us. We implore you on Christ's behalf: Be reconciled to God.

Judging is loving even with people who think they are Christians. Far from shutting you up, any Christian worth the name will welcome your love to help them live poor in spirit. Listen to the Bible in Hebrews 3:12-13, Galatians 3:1 & 6:1, I John 5:16 and Jude 23.

See to it, brothers, that none of you has a sinful, unbelieving heart that turns away from the living God. But encourage one another daily, as long as it is called Today, so that none of you may be hardened by sin's deceitfulness.

You foolish Galatians! Who has bewitched you?

Brothers, if someone is caught in a sin, you who are spiritual should restore him gently. But watch yourself, or you also may be tempted.

If anyone sees his brother commit a sin that does not lead to death, he should pray and God will give him life. I refer to those whose sin does not lead to death. There is a sin that leads to death. I am not saying that he should pray about that. All wrongdoing is sin, and there is sin that does not lead to death.

Be merciful to those who doubt; snatch others from the fire and save them; to others show mercy, mixed with fear—hating even the clothing stained by corrupted flesh.

These Scriptures are saying that you have an appointed part in their salvation. Shall you then fear people taking offense? Shall we not rather fear not helping them awaken from sin's fog? It may be natural to you to fear offending people. That is not wrong; in its proper place it is beneficial in society. But when that fear shuts us up, we are in disagreement with God.

Peter encourages us to speak up by lining up our fears properly, in I Peter 3:14-15.

"Do not fear what they fear; do not be frightened." But in your hearts set apart Christ as Lord. Always be prepared to give an answer to everyone who asks you to give the reason for the hope that you have. But do this with gentleness and respect, keeping a clear conscience...

So far we've had some correction to our thinking in this chapter. This corrected thinking eliminates our cultural bias. It is loving to help people identify and repent for their barriers to God.

It's important now to marry both our new freedom for speaking the truth and the heart of Jesus to love mercifully. He was so amazing, He could communicate love even as He judged. Imagine—the people He excoriated so soundly as children of hell, He later invited to single out one sin He had committed, in John 8:46.

Can any of you prove me guilty of sin? If I am telling the truth, why don't you believe me?

Would you extend such a challenge to those who know you? I think not. As stated, we have much maturity to gain concerning judging in love. Dear reader, this chapter is not a license to correct people but to seek God for what He would say. Yes, we hunger and thirst for righteousness, and the very next Beatitude is that we are merciful.

Another important wisdom about judging within your own church body is to submit your judgments to those in authority over you. The danger of gossip always exists otherwise, a danger which poisons entire church bodies. Those in authority in your fellowship can give you the guidance that God has already imparted to them. They are also in a position to have a fuller picture than you. God will test you to see if you are faithful to obey, even if the discernment He gives you goes nowhere after you hand it off to those in authority.

After all, your best and highest work is to ask God, not talk to others, so rule with your will and your words in the best and most effective way—intercede for those whom God calls to your judging attention.

God doesn't give you His eye into other people so you can fix them or do something about it or call out the posse. He's not doing it to show everyone you are right and wise and should be recognized. He gives you His discernment into a person so you and He can walk in agreement for that person to grow and mature into their appointed freedom. As you walk in agreement with Him for that person, you do so silently, until He gives you something to say. This was Jesus' method in John 8:26-28 and you must follow it.

"I have much to say in judgment of you. But he who sent me is reliable, and what I have heard from him I tell the world."

They did not understand that he was telling them about his Father. So Jesus said, "When you have lifted up the Son of Man, then you will know that I am the one I claim to be and that I do nothing on my own but speak just what the Father has taught me.

God didn't relinquish His command of conviction and attraction when He made you its carrier. He is often doing these things without our even knowing it. When we do perceive His activity in this way, obedience and hearkening to the voice of the Lord are required. When He says speak, you wait and listen for how to speak. When He doesn't say speak, you don't speak.

So what are you, Christian? You are a walking, talking zone of God's continual convicting and attracting.

Apostle Paul conveyed this using a common militaristic image of his day. When Roman commanders would capture new territories that had resisted, they made a public spectacle of the captives by parading them through the streets. The parade used strong incense that carried an aroma to the crowd. Those who had cooperated with Rome were to be spared, and those who had resisted, executed. Paul says we are that aroma in II Corinthians 2:14-16.

But thanks be to God, who always leads us in triumphal procession in Christ and through us spreads everywhere the fragrance of the knowledge of him. For we are to God the aroma of Christ among those who are being saved and those who are perishing. To the one we are the smell of death; to the other, the fragrance of life.

The Bible says you and I and our new race are a signal to everyone on earth, in Philippians 1:28.

This is a sign to them that they will be destroyed, but that you will be saved—and that by God.

Jesus plainly thinks of us this way. Here's what He said in Matthew 5:14-16. It comes right after His Beatitudes where we learned that our poverty of spirit is the most blessed spiritual situation.

You are the light of the world. A city on a hill cannot be hidden. Neither do people light a lamp and put it under a bowl. Instead they put it on its stand, and it gives light to everyone in the house. In the same way, let your light shine before men, that they may see your good deeds and praise your Father in heaven.

Our new race is a collective sign on the earth to unbelievers and those who are Christians in name or idea only. Psalm 14:5 answers why people act funny around you sometimes for reasons you haven't previously been able to figure out.

Will evildoers never learn—
  those who devour my people as men eat bread
  and who do not call on the LORD?
There they are, overwhelmed with dread,
  for God is present in the company of the righteous.

Apostle Paul says so also in Philippians 2:15-16 in his description of us.

children of God without fault in a crooked and depraved generation, in which you shine like stars in the universe as you hold out the word of life

We speak in tongues. One reason God surprised us with that on Pentecost is as a sign to the earth that we are His favored people and that people can be saved if they become one of us. I Corinthians 14:22 says, *Tongues, then, are a sign, not for believers but for unbelievers.* Paul there quotes Isaiah 28:10-11 where God says our speaking in tongues leaves people without excuse and further obscures the truth to which they were unwilling to listen.

> *Very well then, with foreign lips and strange tongues*
> *God will speak to this people,*
> *to whom he said,*
> *"This is the resting place, let the weary rest";*
> *and, "This is the place of repose"—*
> *but they would not listen.*

Not only are you a walking, talking zone of convicting and attracting, you are—with me and our entire new race—a sign to all demons, devils, angels and to every unseen spirit of every kind, according to Ephesians 2:6-7, 3:9-10 and Revelation 12:10-12. We are already in the heavenly realm as a showpiece, as an announcement, as God's timer for the final destruction of evil.

> *And God raised us up with Christ and seated us with him in the heavenly realms in Christ Jesus, in order that in the coming ages he might show the incomparable riches of his grace, expressed in his kindness to us in Christ Jesus.*

> *His [God's] intent was that now, through the church, the manifold wisdom of God should be made known to the rulers and authorities in the heavenly realms.*

> *the accuser of our brothers,*
> *who accuses them before our God day and night,*
> *has been hurled down.*

They overcame him
  by the blood of the Lamb
  and by the word of their testimony;
they did not love their lives so much
  as to shrink from death.
Therefore rejoice, you heavens
  and you who dwell in them!
But woe to the earth and the sea,
  because the devil has gone down to you!
He is filled with fury,
  because he knows that his time is short.

Since we are God's timer for the doom of His enemies, you can see why they aggressively try to confuse us with lies, with poor thinking about ourselves, and with inferiority. Blindfolds are about all they have to work with. The slower we go, the slower we grow, the longer they roam.

In our book, we've established from Scripture that God the Holy Spirit lives in you and me and in each member of Jesus' Bride. (Wow! Is that ever amazing? Hallelujah, Father, what an amazing plan You made up.) As we have seen, the NT writers saw this as the end result for which God sent the gospel and for which Jesus died, rose and ascended (Acts 2:38-39).

So God lives in you, like His headquarters on earth (I Corinthians 6:19-20). Jesus told us what the Holy Spirit would do on earth, from this headquarters in you and me, in John 16:7-11. Like America has a constitution, you could think of this as your constitution as a new creation.

When he comes, he will convict the world of guilt in regard to sin and righteousness and judgment: in regard to sin, because men do not believe in me; in regard to righteousness, because I am going to the Father, where you can see me no longer; and

in regard to judgment, because the prince of this world now
stands condemned.

Wait a minute now. From where does the Holy Spirit convict the world? From the air? From the ground? Through wires? NO—through you. You are a walking, talking convicting influence everywhere you go, every person you meet, whatever you do—because you are a carrier of the Chief Convicter and the Chief Attracter.

What is attractive about what you carry within you? What the Holy Spirit wants to achieve is the desire of all men's hearts: people to know God, and God to live in them as He does in us. Conviction demolishes the strongholds which oppose these breakthroughs, the arguments that keep us oppressed as stated in II Corinthians 10:3-5. In their place floods the power and love of the most wonderful Father. Pitiful self-reliance is fully exposed as a path of failure and destruction. Blindfolds are ripped off and recovery of sight comes to the blind. Listen again to His love in Isaiah 57:15.

Build up, build up, prepare the road!
  Remove the obstacles out of the way of my people."
For this is what the high and lofty One says—
  he who lives forever, whose name is holy:
"I live in a high and holy place,
  but also with him who is contrite and lowly in spirit,
to revive the spirit of the lowly
  and to revive the heart of the contrite.

Isn't that something you want to be part of? Yes, that is your heart and mine. And He announces our role in the first two lines. That's why sharing the gospel, why testifying to our deliverance by God, brings us so much joy. Each time is an excursion out of the fog of fearing people more than God. It's you being rescued from fearing peoples' offense, from the fog-lies of the enemy to shut you up. It's a birth into who you are made to be and into who you really are.

Truth is, 90% of the time, you find that the people you encounter really want what you have and they respond to the Holy Spirit in you with desire. That's your new normal, Mr. Attractant. That's your new normal, Ms. Ambassador. That's the new normal for our entire race.

You are the one who builds up the road and removes the obstacles so God can show Himself to a person. You're poor in spirit, right? So you have no power to reveal God to someone. Your power to reveal is limited to yourself. Likewise, only God can reveal Himself to a person. But He has appointed that you and I prepare the way for that to happen. That's our job. Peter says so in I Peter 2:9,12.

You are a chosen people, a royal priesthood, a holy nation, a people belonging to God, that you may declare the praises of him who called you out of darkness into his wonderful light.... Live such good lives among the pagans that, though they accuse you of doing wrong, they may see your good deeds and glorify God on the day he visits us.

Do you remember what John the Baptist's job was? Matthew 3:1-3 tells us.

In those days John the Baptist came, preaching in the Desert of Judea and saying, "Repent, for the kingdom of heaven is near." This is he who was spoken of through the prophet Isaiah: "A voice of one calling in the desert, 'Prepare the way for the Lord, make straight paths for him.'"

So far so good, that's John the Baptist and it was long ago but no—listen to what Jesus says about you compared to John the Baptist in Matthew 11:11.

I tell you the truth: Among those born of women there has not risen anyone greater than John the Baptist; yet he who is least in the kingdom of heaven is greater than he.

ACTIVATION 9-3

Using only what you've read in this chapter, write out statements about yourself and other followers of Jesus that begin with the two words, "I am." You can use the phrases from the chapter title to help.

I am _____

I am _____

I am _____

ACTIVATION 9-4

In II Thessalonians 2:10-12 Apostle Paul says there are only two loves, only two delights—to love the truth, or, to delight in wickedness.

They perish because they refused to love the truth and so be saved. For this reason God sends them a powerful delusion so that they will believe the lie and so that all will be condemned who have not believed the truth but have delighted in wickedness.

Look back on the names you listed earlier in this chapter. List them again below. Then, using your spiritual perception of their spiritual situation, draw a line from each name to a point on the scale below.

Delighting├────┼────┼────┼────┼────┼────┼────┤ Loving
in wickedness   the truth

_____
_____
_____

_____

Circle each one above who has any delight at all in wickedness. Write a prayer for them in these next lines below.

_____

_____

_____

_____

_____

Last, in the blanks below, write out for practice things you could verbally say to them.

_____

_____

_____

_____

_____

Christian! You and your race are a zone of attraction and conviction. Every place you go, every phone call, every work encounter, every conversation, every stop at public places—God placed you in it to prepare the way for Him. Loosen your lips, get ready and be alert!

God! I take off my blindfold that prevented me from judging sin.
Thank you for letting me work with people
to forsake sin and love You.

CHAPTER 10:
YOU ARE AN EARTH-RULER, AND PHYSICAL REALITY IS READY TO RESPOND TO YOU AND GOD IN YOU

Earlier we reviewed Scripture that shows you to be a Spirit-dominant creature. In this chapter we turn our attention to what your spirit dominates.

ACTIVATION 10-1

Describe a time that physical reality made way for you. For instance, natural law was slowed or suspended; a disaster that should have occurred did not; or, a physical accomplishment was easier than it should have been. Perhaps it was a healing, or a business transaction.

_____

_____

_____

_____

Describe a time that you have seen prayer change physical reality.

_____

_____

_____

_____

ACTIVATION 10-2

Is there anyone you know who seems to have a consistent or surprising mastery over physical reality? Write their names below.

1. _____

2. _____

3. _____

4. _____

ACTIVATION 10-3

Have you ever dreamed—night dream or day dream—that physical reality did what you wanted? If so, jot down a brief phrase to identify what happened.

_____

_____

ACTIVATION 10-4

In chapter 6, we showed that the transactional viewpoint was unbiblical. It assesses your quantity of faith. Your view was transformed because we replaced it in your head with the confidence relationship. Write below some changes that have occurred in you since then.

_____

_____

_____

_____

_____

_____

ACTIVATION 10-5

Now let's take it a step further. Our book's subject is what you are, and that is an identity question. Remember when Jesus calmed the storm in Mark 4:39-41? Let's say you are in the boat with him and the disciples. Jesus is in that sinking boat with you, with a ferocious storm threatening to kill you all. Then Jesus speaks and calms the storm.

What do you think or say after that?

_____

_____

_____

_____

People in our society might have these responses. "How did he do that?" "Show me how you do that!" "What exactly did he say to do that? That's the formula!" "We can use this to get a big church going!" "Everyone else needs to know that he can do this!" A few might even say, "thank you!"

The record in Mark 4:39-41 shows the 12 disciples in the boat said none of these.

They were terrified and asked each other, "Who is this? Even the wind and the waves obey him!"

They utter an identity question: Who is this? And Scripture teaches us that, with physical reality, the question of identity is the main question—not "how much faith you have" as the transactional viewpoint says.

Let's jump back 1,200 years to Moses in Exodus 4:1-3.

Moses answered, "What if they do not believe me or listen to me and say, 'The LORD did not appear to you'?" Then the LORD said to him, "What is that in your hand?" "A staff," he replied. The LORD said, "Throw it on the ground." Moses threw it on the ground and it became a snake, and he ran from it. Then the LORD said to him, "Reach out your hand and take it by the tail." So Moses reached out and took hold of the snake and it turned back into a staff in his hand. "This," said the LORD, "is so that they may believe that the LORD, the God of their fathers—the God of Abraham, the God of Isaac and the God of Jacob—has appeared to you."

Okay, a whoop-tee-do sign is how you may have read that in the past, and thought it had no present significance for you. This may be one of the many surprising truths saved in Scripture for your maturity & readiness. After all, how does God figure that a staff becoming a snake, which even Pharaoh's magicians could do, would be effective to convince the mass of enslaved Hebrews that He appeared to Moses? Was God caught off guard by the competencies of the Egyptian magicians? No of course, so there is more than meets the Western eye here.

The staff was least of all a tool to lean on. Moses was an experienced and vigorous shepherd in extremely rugged country. He was definitely not a tottering old man in need of support. When he came down with the two stone tablets, they definitely would have been heavy. Even when he died 40 years later, Moses was so vigorous he climbed a high mountain to die there!

The staff was symbol of authority, much as we would regard a king's scepter. In Greek mythology, did Neptune need his trident? No, it symbolized his authority and even today some cruise ships sail under it.

The staff was held by the hand. "Stretching out my staff" came to have a shorthand equivalent, "stretch out my hand." Let's see how God regarded Moses' staff, which He enabled Moses to turn into a snake on command.

> The LORD said to Moses and Aaron, "When Pharaoh says to you, 'Perform a miracle,' then say to Aaron, 'Take your staff and throw it down before Pharaoh,' and it will become a snake." So Moses and Aaron went to Pharaoh and did just as the LORD commanded. Aaron threw his staff down in front of Pharaoh and his officials, and it became a snake. (Exodus 7:8-10)

> "Wait on the bank of the Nile to meet him, and take in your hand the staff that was changed into a snake." ..The LORD said to Moses, "Tell Aaron, 'Take your staff and stretch out your hand over the waters of Egypt...and they will turn to blood. Blood will be everywhere in Egypt..." Moses and Aaron did just as the LORD had commanded. He raised his staff in the presence of Pharaoh and his officials and struck the water of the Nile, and all the water was changed into blood. (7:14,18-20)

*Then the L*ORD *said to Moses, "Tell Aaron, 'Stretch out your hand with your staff over the streams and canals and ponds, and make frogs come up on the land of Egypt.'" So Aaron stretched out his hand over the waters of Egypt, and the frogs came up and covered the land. (8:5-6)*

*Then the L*ORD *said to Moses, "Tell Aaron, 'Stretch out your staff and strike the dust of the ground,' and throughout the land of Egypt the dust will become gnats." They did this, and when Aaron stretched out his hand with the staff and struck the dust of the ground, gnats came upon men and animals. (8:16-17)*

*Then the L*ORD *said to Moses, "Stretch out your hand toward the sky so that hail will fall all over Egypt—on men and animals and on everything growing in the fields of Egypt." When Moses stretched out his staff toward the sky, the L*ORD *sent thunder and hail, and lightning flashed down to the ground....Then Moses left Pharaoh and went out of the city. He spread out his hands toward the L*ORD*; the thunder and hail stopped, and the rain no longer poured down on the land. (9:22-23, 33)*

*And the L*ORD *said to Moses, "Stretch out your hand over Egypt so that locusts will swarm over the land and devour everything growing in the fields, everything left by the hail." So Moses stretched out his staff over Egypt, and the L*ORD *made an east wind blow across the land all that day and all that night. By morning the wind had brought the locusts. (10:12-13)*

*Then the L*ORD *said to Moses, "Stretch out your hand toward the sky so that darkness will spread over Egypt—darkness that can be felt." So Moses stretched out his hand toward the sky, and total darkness covered all Egypt for three days. (10:21-22)*

Clearly God had a purpose for Moses' staff. It wasn't a magic wand. In the hand of Moses, it expressed to all of physical reality the authority of God placed upon Moses. With it He activated 6 of the 10 plagues by Moses' and Aaron's outstretched staff. "Moses is an Earth-Ruler," it said.

But the big one was yet to be seen, in Exodus 14:15-16, 21 & 26-27.

> *Then the LORD said to Moses, "Why are you crying out to me? Tell the Hebrews to move on. Raise your staff and stretch out your hand over the sea to divide the water so that the Israelites can go through the sea on dry ground.*
>
> *Then Moses stretched out his hand over the sea, and all that night the LORD drove the sea back with a strong east wind and turned it into dry land. The waters were divided, and the Israelites went through the sea on dry ground, with a wall of water on their right and on their left.*
>
> *Then the LORD said to Moses, "Stretch out your hand over the sea so that the waters may flow back over the Egyptians and their chariots and horsemen." Moses stretched out his hand over the sea, and at daybreak the sea went back to its place. The Egyptians were fleeing toward it, and the LORD swept them into the sea.*

Could God have said, "I will divide the water for you?" Sure, like many a parent who said "Here, let me do it for you." Why didn't He? The role of the staff tells us He had a purpose in establishing Moses' identity & authority. The thing of the earth in Moses' hand was authorized by God to signify Moses' rulership of earth.

Look at the above again. Let's break down the partnership of God and man. Who had the idea? The LORD did. Who actually sent the wind & drove the sea to stand up in walls? The LORD did. By whose will and words and action was the LORD's idea activated? Moses'.

Now did Moses have magical powers? Did his staff emit lightning bolts? That's what our movie-conditioned minds may think. But what we see here is physical reality responding to the authority of a man, and God working within Moses' authority and identity for all physical reality to see.

Let's jump back another long period to our original creation. What we just saw with Moses is consistent with God's announced intent at that time, in Genesis 1:26-28.

Then God said, "Let us make man in our image, in our likeness, and let them rule over the fish of the sea and the birds of the air, over the livestock, over all the earth, and over all the creatures that move along the ground."

So God created man in his own image,
   in the image of God he created him;
   male and female he created them.

God blessed them and said to them, "Be fruitful and increase in number; fill the earth and subdue it. Rule over the fish of the sea and the birds of the air and over every living creature that moves on the ground. "

Look at the original scope of your authority—everything of the earth. And in what pattern are you made? The pattern of God. We, male and female, are His image. We are His likeness. Let's see—that sounds like we represent God. He gave us authority delegated by Him, and mandated that we rule a certain portion of the King's total kingdom. And that certain portion is everything having to do with the earth. In a manner of speaking, we are God to everything we subdue in His name.

Jesus quoted Psalm 82:6 when he spoke to the hostile religious leaders in John 10:33-36.

"We are not stoning you for any of these," replied the Jews, "but for blasphemy, because you, a mere man, claim to be God."

Jesus answered them, "Is it not written in your Law, 'I have said you are gods'? If he called them 'gods,' to whom the word of God came—and the Scripture cannot be broken — what about the one whom the Father set apart as his very own and sent into the world? Why then do you accuse me of blasphemy because I said, 'I am God's Son'?"

He called Himself the Son of Man more frequently than he called Himself the Son of God. The original created identity for man and our original scope of authority was one reason He did so.

Our original authority was first seen in our work. Under our Fall-trained thinking, work is bad, vacation is good. But even a light study of Genesis 1-3 shows that work is part of being in God's likeness and image. The very idea of "work" is welcome to God and to the "God-images" He created. Work is first used about God in 2:2-3.

By the seventh day God had finished the work he had been doing; so on the seventh day he rested from all his work. And God blessed the seventh day and made it holy, because on it he rested from all the work of creating that he had done.

What work did God rest from? The work of creating. The Scripture makes clear God doesn't grow tired or weary (Isaiah 40:28). Why then does the beautiful history of God's creating end with this work and rest emphasis? At least one reason is because like any Father, He patterns behaviors for His children.

How did God do His work of creating? You can review Genesis 1 and you will find no shoveling, no tinkering, no blast furnaces. He spoke His will. That is His pattern, and the next reference to work is about us, His images on site to rule the earth—in Genesis 2:5,15.

no shrub of the field had yet appeared on the earth and no plant of the field had yet sprung up, for the Lḭord God had not sent rain on the earth and there was no man to work the ground....

> *The Lord God took the man and put him in the Garden of Eden*
> *to work it and take care of it.*

Let's check our habitual thinking at the door of Scripture. What is our scope of authority? Everything of earth. What is our pattern of work? Willing and speaking it. So how likely is it the man's work is nothing more than hoeing and raking? After all, there's no mention of hoes and rakes being created. What is the man's work? Pull weeds? Really?

There is work we do in the Garden and it is verbal—naming the animals. The authority of our naming is plainly indicated in Genesis 2:19. *Whatever the man called each living creature, that was its name. That* phrase appears for what purpose? It is our first work, our first ruling act, and its authority is pointedly recognized by God and all creation.

Isn't it obvious that God meant the man to will and to speak the care of the garden?

This interpretation makes sense of the curse upon the ground in 3:17-19. Instead of working by will and words in the Garden, where food was free, the man now has to apply brute, sweaty force at the expense of his ease, comfort and rest.

> *Cursed is the ground because of you;*
> *   through painful toil you will eat of it*
> *   all the days of your life.*
> *It will produce thorns and thistles for you,*
> *   and you will eat the plants of the field.*
> *By the sweat of your brow*
> *   you will eat your food.*

The Scripture has many people whose example to us is repentance, obedience and character. But in addition to them are those who exemplify to us what our original creation authorizes us to be. These are people who foreshadow (as Paul said in Romans 15:4) what our Edenic work pattern can be today.

Joshua was the general of Israel's conquest army. In Joshua 10:12-13, physical reality responded readily to his authority.

> *On the day the LORD gave the Amorites over to Israel, Joshua said to the LORD in the presence of Israel:*
>
> *"O sun, stand still over Gibeon,*
> *O moon, over the Valley of Aijalon. "*
> *So the sun stood still,*
> *and the moon stopped,*
> *till the nation avenged itself on its enemies,*
>
> *as it is written in the Book of Jashar. The sun stopped in the middle of the sky and delayed going down about a full day.*

Elijah and Elisha star during a period of dramatic displays of authority over physical reality. Consider this list of the masteries exhibited at that time over physical creation.

I Kings 17:1, over rain, to produce nationwide drought

17:14, to produce self-replenishing food (in direct contravention of the curse)

17:21, over death, to resurrect a dead person

18:36-38, to produce fire from the sky

18:41-43, over rain, to end nationwide drought

22:23, over life, to pronounce death for a king

II Kings 1:4, over life, to pronounce death for a king

1:10, to produce fire from the sky

1:12, to produce fire from the sky

2:8, to part a river into dry ground

2:11, a chariot of fire from the sky

2:22, to change salt water to fresh

2:24, to command bears

3:17,20, to fill a desert with water everywhere in sight
4:3-5, to multiply commercially salable olive oil
4:34, over death, to resurrect a dead person
4:41, to eliminate poison from food
4:43-44, to multiply food
5:14, to heal a leper
6:6, to float sunken iron
6:9, to know distant events
6:18, over sight, to blind a large army
7:1-12, to lift a famine
7:2, to pronounce death for a mocker
8:1, to impose a famine
13:21, over death, to resurrect the dead, even after one's death.

Was that just them? Is the time past and done, when God anointed human beings to dominate physical reality? Jesus didn't think so. Quite the contrary. He spoke as if His arrival signaled the appearing of more and more such individuals.

Otherwise, why would He have rebuked the disciples for having little faith as He did in Mark 4:39-40? He would not have rebuked them, unless He considered they had authority to deal with the problem without waking Him up in fear. Jesus sees them as earth-rulers as much as He is.

He got up, rebuked the wind and said to the waves, "Quiet! Be still!" Then the wind died down and it was completely calm. He said to his disciples, "Why are you so afraid? Do you still have no faith?"

If in fact God is re-activating our dominance over the earth, if in fact God masters physical reality through our rulership, and by our will and our words—then numerous puzzling passages are compellingly explained. We can start with the dramatic and teasing run-up to one of Jesus' most public "miracles" (read, "new normal") in Mark 6:35-38.

> By this time it was late in the day, so his disciples came to him. "This is a remote place," they said, "and it's already very late. Send the people away so they can go to the surrounding countryside and villages and buy themselves something to eat."
>
> But he answered, "You give them something to eat."
>
> They said to him, "That would take eight months of a man's wages! Are we to go and spend that much on bread and give it to them to eat?"
>
> "How many loaves do you have?" he asked. "Go and see."
>
> When they found out, they said, "Five—and two fish."

In the past, haven't you felt some unfairness or perhaps some taunting in Jesus telling them to feed these many people? Certainly the disciples were incredulous. The disciples hear it as Fall-trained people who expect to work eight months to accomplish such a feat. How can Jesus lay this unrealistic expectation on them? Is He trying to frustrate them?

No. Jesus is teaching by challenge. God said to Moses in Exodus 14:15, *Why are you crying out to me?* as if to say, "Moses, you've got the authority." Jesus likewise assumes that His disciples actually have the authority to use five loaves and two fishes to feed 5,000 men with their families. In this "miracle," Jesus is taking them (and us) back before the Fall to the original normal.

In the past, we wanted to skip the time requirement that God built into maturity. Many are those Christians who sought to step directly into their rulership on their own timetable. People get hurt when we do that. It's true that physical reality is ready right now to submit to your rule, according to Romans 8:19-21—but are you ready to rule it?

Ecclesiastes 10:5-6 expresses a foolishness that God doesn't practice:

There is an evil I have seen under the sun, the sort of error that arises from a ruler: Fools are put in many high positions...

Jesus teaches by a process of demanding challenges, because He won't put a fool in rulership. These challenges provoke us to arise to who we are. We follow Him, we watch what He does, we accept His corrections, and we speak and act as He instructs. His testing of us and our obedience in the tests turns us into fit rulers. His tests make us, not simply right, but right in our hearts.

Jesus is fully man, not only fully God. He showed rulership of earth before He was resurrected, not after—showing what a son of man is capable of. He is resurrected so that with our spiritual perception today, we can learn from Him how to rule the earth. And He poured out His Holy Spirit so that we can have the heart to do so.

So we are maturing into our domination of the earth. The expression of that is different among people and places. Some places and people have healing miracles in abundance. Others have spiritual perception of uncommon degree. Others can forgo money yet have plenty. The process and the challenges vary. You can't look down on anyone who hasn't gone through your process. You aren't less a beloved of God if you haven't gone through theirs. What did Paul say in I Corinthians 12:7? *Now to each one the manifestation of the Spirit is given for the common good.*

Whatever the rulership function God ordains for you, we all have the magnetic pointer in us—a vestigial compass to our creation mandate. Dogs have a do-claw on their upper forelegs which plays no role but perhaps once did. It is called vestigial. We have a vestigial recognition of our authority over earth. Unlike the do-claw, however, our authority is being activated.

Jesus speaks to his disciples as if they are like Elijah and Elisha, who multiplied physical resources supernaturally by will and by words. I have been putting "miracles" in quotes because Jesus considered them your normal, and not rare at all. He knew that dominance over physical reality is our birthright, and much more than "divine intervention."

This modern concept of divine intervention is another mutation of a biblical truth. Yes, God intervenes, but not unilaterally. As we saw in Genesis 1:26-28, He gave rulership of the earth to the race of men. If He wants to intervene on earth, He seeks Jesus-followers to agree with Him because it is us recreated human beings that physical reality has been waiting for. Physical reality submitted to a man, the Son of Man and first of many of us.

The feeding of the 5,000 is not the only time Jesus pressures the disciples with mankind's pre-Fall authority. In Mark 8:17-21, as they go in a boat having forgotten food, the disciples misunderstand Jesus' warning about the religious leadership, and as a result they take Jesus to be referring to physical food.

The disciples had forgotten to bring bread, except for one loaf they had with them in the boat. "Be careful," Jesus warned them. "Watch out for the yeast of the Pharisees and that of Herod."

They discussed this with one another and said, "It is because we have no bread."

Aware of their discussion, Jesus asked them: "Why are you talking about having no bread? Do you still not see or understand? Are your hearts hardened? Do you have eyes but fail to see, and ears but fail to hear? And don't you remember?

When I broke the five loaves for the five thousand, how many basketsful of pieces did you pick up?"

"Twelve," they replied.

"And when I broke the seven loaves for the four thousand, how many basketsful of pieces did you pick up?"

They answered, "Seven."

He said to them, "Do you still not understand?"

What did they "still not see or understand?" That food is again free, that forgetting to bring food is not a limit on Jesus or on us, and that with such freedom we devote our attention to heavenly things.

This is affirmed by Jesus' post-feeding remarks recorded by Apostle John in John 6:26-29.

Jesus answered, "I tell you the truth, you are looking for me, not because you saw miraculous signs but because you ate the loaves and had your fill. Do not work for food that spoils, but for food that endures to eternal life, which the Son of Man will give you. On him God the Father has placed his seal of approval."

Then they asked him, "What must we do to do the works God requires?"

Jesus answered, "The work of God is this: to believe in the one he has sent."

Again we hear God defining work as totally something different from our post-Fall thinking. Jesus is the second Adam and is reversing Adam's curse, and restoring authority to men. This is clearly what His hearers understood to be happening in the synagogue of Matthew 9:6-8.

> *But so that you may know that the Son of Man has authority on earth to forgive sins..." Then he said to the paralytic, "Get up, take your mat and go home." And the man got up and went home. When the crowd saw this, they were filled with awe; and they praised God, who had given such authority to men.*

Previously in our workbook we've considered Mark 11:20-25. That's where the disciples are amazed Jesus withered the fig tree by His words. Let's review it again with this recognition that Jesus is reversing the work-is-hard curse upon Adam, and restoring our Edenic pattern of work by will and by words.

> *In the morning, as they went along, they saw the fig tree withered from the roots. Peter remembered and said to Jesus, "Rabbi, look! The fig tree you cursed has withered!"*
> *"Have faith in God," Jesus answered. "I tell you the truth, if anyone says to this mountain, 'Go, throw yourself into the sea,' and does not doubt in his heart but believes that what he says will happen, it will be done for him. Therefore I tell you, whatever you ask for in prayer, believe that you have received it, and it will be yours."*

In normal everyday conversation patterns, we would expect that Jesus responds to their amazement with further commentary on withering fig-trees. But Jesus blows past that subject to something unimaginably big, much greater than tending a garden. Moving mountains is much more impossible than withering a fig-tree, in our Fall-trained thinking. But to Jesus, it is one and the same for us, neither harder than the other. By this He communicates, either one is well within our original scope of authority—everything of the earth.

Another dear expression of Jesus restoring our authority is Matthew 17:25-27. At least, it was dear to the former tax collector who recorded it.

After Jesus and his disciples arrived in Capernaum, the collectors of the two-drachma tax came to Peter and asked, "Doesn't your teacher pay the temple tax?" "Yes, he does," he replied.

When Peter came into the house, Jesus was the first to speak. "What do you think, Simon?" he asked. "From whom do the kings of the earth collect duty and taxes —from their own sons or from others?" "From others," Peter answered.

"Then the sons are exempt," Jesus said to him. "But so that we may not offend them, go to the lake and throw out your line. Take the first fish you catch; open its mouth and you will find a four-drachma coin. Take it and give it to them for my tax and yours."

By now you recognize the numerous indicators: Jesus saw more authority in us than we have yet relied upon. He pressures us to mature into it. He sees you as an earth-ruler, and He sees that physical reality is ready to respond to you and to God in you.

Jesus did not only express this as an assumption. He plainly taught it in passages such as John 14:12, before His death, and in Mark 16:17-18, after His resurrection.

I tell you the truth, anyone who has faith in me will do what I have been doing. He will do even greater things than these, because I am going to the Father.

These signs will accompany those who believe: In my name they will drive out demons; they will speak in new tongues; they will pick up snakes with their hands; and when they drink

deadly poison, it will not hurt them at all; they will place their
hands on sick people, and they will get well.

Ultimately, the Apostles accepted this identity and authority,
after the Holy Spirit was poured out. You and I also can do no less
than accept what Jesus says about us. One of the earliest, most
dramatic occurrences is in Acts 3:6-8.

Then Peter said, "Silver or gold I do not have, but what I have
I give you. In the name of Jesus Christ of Nazareth, walk."
Taking him by the right hand, he helped him up, and instantly
the man's feet and ankles became strong. He jumped to his feet
and began to walk. Then he went with them into the temple
courts, walking and jumping, and praising God.

Earth itself responded to the apostles in Acts 4:31.

After they prayed, the place where they were meeting was
shaken. And they were all filled with the Holy Spirit and spoke
the word of God boldly.

Ezekiel had experienced spiritual transportation that changed
his physical location, and so did Philip, in Acts 8:39-40.

When they came up out of the water, the Spirit of the Lord
suddenly took Philip away, and the eunuch did not see him
again, but went on his way rejoicing. Philip, however, appeared
at Azotus...

Peter, like Elijah and Elisha, pronounced death upon a person,
in Acts 5:9.

Peter said to her, "How could you agree to test the Spirit of the
Lord? Look! The feet of the men who buried your husband are

*at the door, and they will carry you out also." At that moment
she fell down at his feet and died.*

And like them, as we are authorized to do, Peter raised someone
from the dead in Acts 9:41.

Paul also raised people from the dead, such as Eutychus in Acts
20:9-11.

*Seated in a window was a young man named Eutychus, who
was sinking into a deep sleep as Paul talked on and on. When
he was sound asleep, he fell to the ground from the third story
and was picked up dead. Paul went down, threw himself on the
young man and put his arms around him. "Don't be alarmed,"
he said. "He's alive!" Then he went upstairs again and broke
bread and ate. After talking until daylight, he left. The people
took the young man home alive and were greatly comforted.*

In view of these things, it is no surprise Peter's shadow (Acts
5:15) and Paul's handkerchiefs (Acts 19:11-12) were alone sufficient
to convey the authority of the men themselves. In a passage that
speaks of those who fell away, Hebrews 6:5 describes them as people
who have tasted the powers of the coming age. This hints at the
mastery and dominance that the early Christians witnessed.

These occurrences were commonplace enough that the Bible
explains Jesus' authority from His ascended position, in Colossians
1:16-17 and Hebrews 1:3.

*For by him all things were created: things in heaven and on
earth, visible and invisible, whether thrones or powers or
rulers or authorities; all things were created by him and for
him. He is before all things, and in him all things hold together.*

The Son is the radiance of God's glory and the exact representation of his being, sustaining all things by his powerful word.

These assert that our authority over the earth comes from Jesus' will and words. In Romans 5, Paul says Adam's race in its fallen position cannot reverse the curse. But the authority of the second Adam permeates His followers who are in partnership with Him, just as we saw the LORD partnering with Moses. The new race of men is in Jesus. That's why we *reign in life* according to Paul's simple analogy in Romans 5:17.

For if, by the trespass of the one man, death reigned through that one man, how much more will those who receive God's abundant provision of grace and of the gift of righteousness reign in life through the one man, Jesus Christ.

Our rulership of earth has its activation in the Holy Spirit's presence in us, its authorization in Jesus' victory, and its origin in the Father's Creation mandate to us. The 24/7 praise in heaven's throne room repeats this continually in Revelation 4:11—God created everything, and He *continues* to create and hold up everything.

You are worthy, our Lord and God,
*   to receive glory and honor and power,*
for you created all things,
*   and by your will they were created*
*   and have their being.*

It's noteworthy the Greek word for "all things" signified not merely tangible physical objects and substances, as we read in our materialistic thinking, but arrangements of them. In other words, situations, timings, coordination, and what we might call "coincidence" are each covered by the term "all things."

And this is who has authorized us in Genesis 1:26 as follows:

Then God said, "Let us make man in our image, in our likeness, and let them rule over the fish of the sea and the birds of the air, over the livestock, over all the earth, and over all the creatures that move along the ground."

It requires a strong defiant will to interpret our authority as limited when so many plainly stated authorizations have been given in Scripture.

How effective is our authorization? Consider this: few of the rulership acts we have seen in Scripture result from what we would call "praying." By far the majority are the simple verbal expression of will and words by a man who is in agreement with God.

We end at the apex of this subject, Paul's description of your relationship with physical creation in Romans 8:19-21. It's a passage you might never have studied carefully. You might have filed it in the post-Fall filing system of your beliefs. With all the Scriptures we reviewed, it will certainly have new depth for you.

The creation waits in eager expectation for the sons of God to be revealed. For the creation was subjected to frustration, not by its own choice, but by the will of the one who subjected it, in hope that the creation itself will be liberated from its bondage to decay and brought into the glorious freedom of the children of God. We know that the whole creation has been groaning as in the pains of childbirth right up to the present time.

Read the first sentence again. Are you born again, and a son (child) of God? Is it evident in the heavenly realms that you are a son of God? Ephesians 2:6 suggests it is. If so, then the above conditions of creation's liberation have been fulfilled. That is a deeply consequential event.

You, Christian, are what creation has been eagerly expecting. Remember, the Church is God's clock. Everything He made is watching us to know what is going on and how much time is left.

In these comments, Paul describes creation as having expectations and frustrations, pains and desires, bondage and liberty, decay and freedom. Perhaps you dismissed this as the literary technique of personification, which fits our materialistic education. We know the Bible accurately reveals what God has done, according to the genre of the passage or book of the Bible. While Psalms and the Prophets of the Old Testament may do so, Paul doesn't use personification. So doesn't it seem more likely that Paul is teaching us an actual kind of liveliness God instilled into the creation that He made? It certainly fits with everything we have seen in Scripture.

Creation has a frustrated purpose. What is that purpose? to respond readily to our will and our words as God's images on the earth. Creation seeks its proper rule—by the creature originally mandated to rule it, you and your new race. It is ready to respond to you and to God in you..

Our will and our words aren't only "do this, do that." We are the designated "first responders" to the Glory of God. Imagine you have witnessed an accident where people were hurt. Without the tools and training, you are hesitant to move them or treat them. You are waiting on the first responders—the ambulance or firemen—who are designated, equipped and trained. In the same way, creation waits on us to arrive as the first responders, activating what God wants by our will and our words. Then creation comes into agreement with us, its designated rulers, on whom it must wait.

Thy kingdom come, Thy will be done, on earth as it is in heaven.

Creation was born by will & words, and it was made to be ruled by will and words—those of God's images, sinless mankind, God's deputized authorities. As Paul said, through the one man Jesus we reign in life, sinless under His Redemption.

God bound creation to decay since the first Adam chose death. But the second Adam chose life and we are in Him. What should be happening now? Creation awakes under our feet. As God said at Babel, *nothing will be impossible for them.* We reign in life.

In helping us think this way, the church has received a grand legacy from British authors George MacDonald, Charles Williams, C.S. Lewis and J.R.R. Tolkien. The popularity of these books stems in part from their recognition of our vestigial authority to rule by will and words, and of earth submitting to that rule. All their tales depict tested men ruling creation, and physical reality responding to them. What the authors' contemporaries were not ready for, they put into story form for us, who would one day arise with understanding, us who would endure our tests and become fit to rule.

If you can accept this biblical thinking, there are many Bible truths on the other side of it—Bible truths you can discover, test and use in everyday life. Think of the implications. This truth affects your income, your housekeeping, your yard work, your church ministries, your evangelism—everything within your authority that He gives you.

ACTIVATION 10-6

Write down below areas of physical creation that you have already begun desiring to dominate.

1. _____

2. _____

3. _____

4. _____

The Bible makes your authority very plain. Write down how you can verbally express your authority in the areas you just indicated.

For area 1. _____

For area 2. _____

_____

For area 3. _____

_____

For area 4. _____

_____

Our dominion over creation is practical. Just as the staff expressed Moses' authority, and the shadow conveyed Peter's and the handkerchiefs conveyed Paul's, so also you can delegate your authority and identity through actions and objects. For instance, how many women have prayed blessings over letters to their distant loved ones? It is no accident that prayer shawls and the like are rising in prominence at this time.

When I am interceding and desire a broader discernment, I sometimes ask God what creation holds. Perceiving what creation says is biblical. It is as if creation is one of God's recorders, a library of all the acts of men, and at His direction releases things for our perception and effectiveness at releasing people from oppression. Genesis 4:10-11 and Psalm 19:1-4 are two examples.

As earth-rulers, we can instruct creation to cooperate in matters governed by God's agreements with us. "Be calm!" "Go, throw yourself into the sea!" These are biblical instructions to creation, for just two examples.

What differentiates Christian practice and Scriptural teaching about this from the witchcraft of darkness is the source and conduct of the authority. There are forgers and counterfeiters but we don't stop using money. Likewise, misusers of mankind's creation authority don't force us to forfeit our rulership. To the contrary, we are instructed to resist them, to expose them, and to prove stronger than they are. Paul's contest with Elymas the sorcerer in Acts 13:10-11 demonstrates this.

Our answer to these counterfeiters is instead that we are vigilant to our own hearts, always walking in the Beatitude attitudes we have discussed.

ACTIVATION 10-7

Write down some action you and your church can use to identify yourself and your authority to the earth that you rule.

1. _____
2. _____
3. _____
4. _____

What are you, Christian? You are an Earth-Ruler. You are the First Responder to God that it has been waiting for. The Earth stands ready to respond to you and to God in you.

Father, thank you for creating me to help rule the earth.
Earth, I call you to the service and honor of Jesus Christ, with me.

CHAPTER 11:
YOU ARE A FEARSOME OPPONENT AND AN UNDEFEATABLE CONQUEROR OF GOD'S ENEMIES, AND YOU ARE THEIR FEARSOME REPLACEMENT

Let's bring out your current feelings about the devil and demons.

ACTIVATION 11-1

☐Yes ☐No Have you ever thought it strange the things Jesus said to the demons?

☐Yes ☐No Have you ever been puzzled by the things they said to Him?

☐Yes ☐No Have you ever wondered where demons were in the Old Testament?

☐Yes ☐No Have you ever worried whether demons were influencing your life?

You are not alone, and for people with one of these questions, the Lord's revelation is awesome relief. Check your answers to the below also.

ACTIVATION 11-2

☐Yes ☐No Can demons bother Christians?

☐Yes ☐No Demons are real.

☐Yes ☐No Demons are more frequent outside America.

☐Yes ☐No I worry about evil forces attacking me.

☐Yes ☐No I feel helpless and exposed to enemy attack and temptation.

☐Yes ☐No Giving any attention to demons makes

things worse.

☐Yes ☐No Demons are more powerful than men.

☐Yes ☐No Demons are active in people and
places I encounter.

ACTIVATION 11-3

Now please fill in the following blanks because we will refer to them later. Write in people's names as follows. First, someone you have known whose problems were so inescapable, repetitive or severe that you wondered if demons were causing them.

_____

_____

_____

Second, a time or times when the presence of evil close to you was inescapably perceptible?

_____

_____

_____

Third, a time or times when you participated in a victory over perceptible evil?

_____

_____

_____

Fourth, someone you would immediately think to seek out for help with an insurmountable evil obstacle?

_____

_____

_____

Last, try to put into words why the person you named stands out as the right person for dealing with perceptible evil.

_____

What are you, Christian?

A clear picture of you has emerged from Scripture through our workbook. Now the last chapter has arrived. Notice that we have covered 10 chapters prior to discussing unseen evil opposition. There are three reasons for that.

The first reason is to counteract the quickness of most American Christians to pay the devil attention. Think of that phrase we have: "pay attention." Let's not pay the devil anything. Does he deserve any attention from us? No, he does not. According to Isaiah 14:19, what ultimately happens to the devil is the total opposite of the prominence his pride sought—he is forgotten and disdained.

The second reason we waited to cover this is to establish in your head your identity, your authority, and your capabilities before we put in your hands a sword you can't handle. This sword isn't too big because your enemies are too big. This sword is impossible to handle for the poor in spirit, and that is God's ordained way.

The third reason is to properly define God's enemies. Lucifer has become satan, the accuser, but still possesses his archangel nature. He governs the kingdom of darkness. But there are other enemies.

One that the Bible speaks of is sin. Sin is a living, personal force within us. Romans 7:7-25 is a passage that describes our wrestle with the enemy of sin. Such talk is a no-no in the American tolerance manual where men are assumed good. Paul's comments about sin can be dismissed as a poetic technique of personification by our materialistic view of life. We also saw this with creation's expressive capabilities in the previous chapter.

The Bible teaches us about another enemy: the world, the present world-system. The collective sin of billions of fallen people over centuries gives birth to a malevolent force that persistently oppresses people and opposes their original created rulership. A phrase used today to describe this is systemic sin.

These three enemies are traditionally known as the world, the flesh and the devil. As spiritual perception increases, perhaps Bible teaching on additional enemies will be understood. These are quite enough, thank you.

Earlier we saw the Biblical necessity to be judging. We are commanded to "see to it." We must distinguish good from evil, in society, in churches (under protocol of our leadership) and in ourselves. This maturity to judge is critical in dealing with our enemies. How are we to know something is from God, or from an enemy? After all, it's actually rare we have a clear choice between good and evil if we have some basic Christian maturity. The attacks we experience are far more subtle choices between listening to God or doing it our way. Often, we may be well within God's Word and God's way but influenced by our enemies on God's timing.

Many Christians are quick to attribute excessive stature to the devil. Sometimes, they don't know their own capabilities, they overestimate their enemies' capabilities, and they try to grunt it out with intensity and seriousness. Other times, they approach the subject with an arrogant quality, the kind rebuked in Jude 8-10.

Consider the lesson of David in I Samuel 17:38-40.

> *Then Saul dressed David in his own tunic. He put a coat of armor on him and a bronze helmet on his head. David fastened on his sword over the tunic and tried walking around, because he was not used to them.*
>
> *"I cannot go in these," he said to Saul, "because I am not used to them." So he took them off. Then he took his staff in his hand, chose five smooth stones from the stream, put them in the pouch of his shepherd's bag and, with his sling in his hand, approached the Philistine.*

Saul and his army had been quaking for 40 days, too afraid to go face Goliath. They try to impose their armor upon David—as if it had held some proven value? David instead takes a sling and five stones. David wisely sees the true resource for his victory in 17:45-47.

> *David said to the Philistine, "You come against me with sword and spear and javelin, but I come against you in the name of the Lord Almighty, the God of the armies of Israel, whom you have defied. This day the Lord will hand you over to me, and I'll strike you down and cut off your head. Today I will give the carcasses of the Philistine army to the birds of the air and the beasts of the earth, and the whole world will know that there is a God in Israel. All those gathered here will know that it is not by sword or spear that the Lord saves; for the battle is the Lord's, and he will give all of you into our hands."*

Same with you. You have the same resource—the God with whom you are in continual communion and rest.

You know as well as I do that many Christians feel powerless before the devil, to whom they attribute an endless omnipotence for causing trouble. They despair about the world's intimidating problems. Neither is biblical. The devil is not all-powerful and the world's problems are not the main thing going on. Rather, this helpless despair, this hanging on til the Rapture, illuminates there is a blindfold to who they really are.

ACTIVATION 11-4

So as usual, we'll look at the right water for your thinking to swim in. Let's benchmark by drawing a line from the three statements to a point on the scale below.

definitely ├──────┼──────┼──────┼──────┼──────┼──────┼──────┤ definitely
don't feel it   have this confidence

1. I am a fearsome opponent of God's enemies.
2. I am an undefeatable conqueror of them.
3. I am their fearsome replacement.

Let's review the present condition of God's unseen enemies, and ourselves as well. Following are Colossians 2:15, I John 3:8, Acts 10:38 & Hebrews 2:14. That's just for starters.

Having disarmed the powers and authorities, he made a public spectacle of them, triumphing over them by the cross.

The reason the Son of God appeared was to destroy the devil's work.

[You know] how God anointed Jesus of Nazareth with the Holy Spirit and power, and how he went around doing good and healing all who were under the power of the devil, because God was with him.

He too [Jesus] shared in their humanity so that by his death he might destroy him who holds the power of death—that is, the devil...

The New Testament clearly states that the devil is in a broken condition. You just read it: instead of being fully functional in his malevolence, the devil and his partners are disarmed. Their power is broken. Their work is being destroyed.

A pastor recently said in my hearing, "People come to me and ask me to pray for them because they are under attack by the devil. I say to them, 'Why did you get under? God set you over.'"

ACTIVATION 11-5

According to those Scriptures, write below some biblical statements about your standing regarding the devil and demons.

_____

_____

_____

_____

_____

This stands in stark contrast to the functional supremacy allowed the devil by many Christians and churches. Why does this mythology of the devil receives so much prominence?

One possible explanation is the relief this blindfold offers. Halfhearted believers want someone else to blame. They themselves resist dying to themselves and truly following Jesus. As a result, they have the problems of having two masters as Jesus warned. Rather than admit their halfheartedness and repent with poverty of spirit that is blessed, they can blame the devil.

Another explanation is that "Christians" can have a non-aggression covenant with the devil. This is amazing—a covenant that they won't oppose him and reduce his preferred stature, if he doesn't bother them. You can hear it in the way we talk: "new levels, new devils" and "don't pray for patience." God sees this and describes such a non-aggression covenant in Isaiah 28:14-15.

> *Therefore hear the word of the LORD, you scoffers*
> *who rule this people in Jerusalem.*
> *You boast, "We have entered into a covenant with death,*
> *with the grave we have made an agreement.*
> *When an overwhelming scourge sweeps by,*
> *it cannot touch us,*
> *for we have made a lie our refuge*
> *and falsehood our hiding place. "*

The unseen enemies were motivated by pride to usurp God's throne, and they continue to be. Consider the self-elevation in this remark the devil made to Jesus in Luke 4:5-7.

> *The devil led him [Jesus] up to a high place and showed him in*
> *an instant all the kingdoms of the world. And he said to him,*

"I will give you all their authority and splendor, for it has been given to me, and I can give it to anyone I want to. So if you worship me, it will all be yours."

The devil's aims are well-served when Christians choose to cower and "get under." Good thing Jesus didn't. What's his attitude? Look at Luke 11:21-22.

When a strong man, fully armed, guards his own house, his possessions are safe. But when someone stronger attacks and overpowers him, he takes away the armor in which the man trusted and divides up the spoils.

It's amazing how Jesus could say so much in so few words. The context makes clear He identifies himself as the "someone stronger." Contrast Him with the demonic forces He is describing. They are fundamentally weak and fearful, like Saul and the frightened Israelites before Goliath, and they need armor. They trust in their armor for defense. They also fully arm themselves offensively, and they maintain a vigilant guard over what they consider their own possession, their own house—people.

Jesus, the "someone stronger," is so much more powerful, that He doesn't need armament for offense. He doesn't need armor for defense. He is completely unaffected by their armament and armor. And before Him, all their weapons and defenses are as nothing. Nothing the strong man can do to guard his house can offer any resistance to Jesus. It's possible Jesus knew this about Himself from Old Testament Scriptures like Isaiah 59:16-18 and Psalm 149:6-9.

Jesus was meek and lowly and now is elevated to an exalted position by God the Father. At neither time did He shrink from His resolve and His authority, nor should His followers. He is strong to fight, and fight He does, to recapture what enemies have taken. He is gathering an army to carry this fight to the gates of Hell. In Matthew 16:18, He said that army is His Church. The Church will fight in His delegated authority. They will bind these enemies, take away the armor in which they trusted, and lay claim to the spoils.

This explains His next statement in Luke 11:23, which otherwise seems out of place: *He who is not with me is against me, and he who does not gather with me, scatters.* The someone stronger has followers who do the same as He does—stripping the armor of the oppressing strong men.

If a person is not doing this with Jesus and His Church, then the net effect is to leave the spoils—people—under the guard of enemies, their possession, isolated and scattered. Jesus says a person is against Him if they are not actively gathering with him. This urges vigilance upon you, hungering and thirsting for righteousness, to be alert and penitent for any covenant you have had with the devil.

I imagine what Jesus was thinking when He heard the devil's boastful taunt in Luke 4:6 that he owned all the earth's kingdoms and could give it to anyone he wanted to: "You just wait. I am taking it back!" It's easy to imagine Jesus drew upon Isaiah 49:24-26.

Can plunder be taken from warriors,
or captives rescued from the fierce?

But this is what the LORD says:

"Yes, captives will be taken from warriors,
and plunder retrieved from the fierce;
I will contend with those who contend with you,
and your children I will save.
I will make your oppressors eat their own flesh;
they will be drunk on their own blood, as with wine.

There are many passages of the Old Testament, where God's anger and ours is well expressed. These are described with the adjective "imprecatory." There we see the anger of God at the enemies' attacks on mankind all these many centuries. And God has a strategy of vengeance upon them.

What is God's strategy to overturn the fallen angels? Mankind. Think of it—God's most fragile creatures, the very poorest in spirit, are God's ordained overthrowers of the rebellious, angelic in their created nature, mighty in spirit though evil.

The first man to bring their doom is Jesus, as Son of Man, as the second Adam. One reason God chose the method of Incarnation is this: only man *should* defeat the devil, but only God *could*. Only man *should* pay for sin, but only God *could*. St. Anselm of Canterbury wrote that in his influential book, *Cur Deus Homo (Why God became Man)* in 1098. That defeat could only be administered by a man who *could* sin but does not. His name is Jesus.

In the desert Satan tried to induce Jesus to disqualify Himself by just the slightest sin. A man who sinned could not satisfy God's wrath or release mankind from the devil's oppression. Once Jesus successfully resisted temptation, the devil's empire crumbled to powerlessness before Him. The creation beheld a second Adam, 100% man who would succeed where Adam had failed.

One Sabbath in a synagogue, the witnessed had this response to Jesus in Mark 1:27.

> *The people were all so amazed that they asked each other, "What is this? A new teaching—and with authority! He even gives orders to evil spirits and they obey him."*

They recognized Jesus' command over demons was not limited to driving them out. Mark records in 1:34 that Jesus could forbid them to speak at all or talk about certain subjects among men.

> *Jesus healed many who had various diseases. He also drove out many demons, but he would not let the demons speak because they knew who he was.*

Consider this event from Mark 5:7-13. Notice the display of mastery by the Second Adam, the Son of man, our Jesus.

> *When he saw Jesus from a distance, he ran and fell on his knees in front of him. He shouted at the top of his voice, "What do you want with me, Jesus, Son of the Most High God? Swear to God that you won't torture me!" For Jesus had said to him, "Come out of this man, you evil spirit!"*
>
> *Then Jesus asked him, "What is your name?"*
>
> *"My name is Legion," he replied, "for we are many." And he begged Jesus again and again not to send them out of the area.*
>
> *A large herd of pigs was feeding on the nearby hillside. The demons begged Jesus, "Send us among the pigs; allow us to go into them." He gave them permission, and the evil spirits came out and went into the pigs.*

The demons considered Jesus their tormentor. When commanded to answer a question, they could not refuse or lie. In Jesus' presence, they are reduced to begging pitifully and powerlessly. They clearly recognize Jesus' authority over where they are permitted to be. This is what being the "someone stronger" looks like, and it is what our effectiveness looks like. The enemies perceive it, all of heaven perceives it, and our blindfolds are being removed to perceive it.

It comes as no surprise therefore that Jesus shows intimate awareness of their habits, in Luke 11:24-26.

> *When an evil spirit comes out of a man, it goes through arid places seeking rest and does not find it. Then it says, 'I will return to the house I left.' When it arrives, it finds the house swept clean and put in order. Then it goes and takes seven other spirits more wicked than itself, and they go in and live there. And the final condition of that man is worse than the first.*

He speaks of the inescapable restlessness they have. He refers to their quickness to associate with other demons. In fact, He reveals there are scales of wickedness among demons; a less wicked one opens doors for more wicked demons. He shows a demon's desire to take back what he once had. And He makes plain their willingness to do whatever it takes to re-capture someone they have lost. How did He know these things? As perfect Son of Man, He had spiritual perception—same as you now do as His follower.

God's strategy is to defeat the enemies through mankind. But Jesus is not just the first to defeat the enemies—He is the first of *many*.

It's noteworthy He only referred to church two times in His earthly ministry. With the Church so prominent in His plan, this makes those two references all the more power-packed. In the first of these He is stating His resolute determination to attack hell and to arrest its demonic citizens. And how? Through the Church race of new creation people, in Matthew 16:18-19.

And I tell you that you are Peter, and on this rock I will build my church, and the gates of Hades will not overcome it. I will give you the keys of the kingdom of heaven; whatever you bind on earth will be bound in heaven, and whatever you loose on earth will be loosed in heaven.

This is forceful, resolute, capable, competent, confident and undefeatable binding. This is not a powerless, sheepish and silly arrest by an apologetic, comfort-preserving Church, as if it were Barney Fife with only one bullet in his shirt pocket, the classic character from TV's Andy Griffith Show. What Jesus said we would do isn't based on knowing doctrines and propositions. It is only possible if His followers and His Church have the same capability He did, to recognize and respond properly to demons in the heavenlies. You see that you do have that capability, with your blindfolds removed.

Of course Jesus is referring not to the new heavens from which all evil enemies are banished, but the heavens in which they exist and even present themselves to God, as Job 1-2 shows. Another example is I Kings 22:19-22.

I saw the LORD sitting on his throne with all the host of heaven standing around him on his right and on his left. And the LORD said, 'Who will entice Ahab into attacking Ramoth Gilead and going to his death there?'

"One suggested this, and another that. Finally, a spirit came forward, stood before the LORD and said, 'I will entice him.'

"'By what means?' the LORD asked.

"'I will go out and be a lying spirit in the mouths of all his prophets,' he said.

"'You will succeed in enticing him,' said the LORD. 'Go and do it.'

"So now the LORD has put a lying spirit in the mouths of all these prophets of yours. The LORD has decreed disaster for you."

While this has mystified many, its understanding is easy now for followers of Jesus who recognize heaven is a realm and it is in dispute by those who oppose God. We are the houses that enemies guard with all the armor they can amass, and all the agreement they can muster among themselves. Mankind is the safely guarded possession of the enemy, consigned to the world, flesh and devil with no escape.

That is, until the action of God through Jesus' death, until our filling with the Holy Spirit. Now an ever-increasing number of men has been transferred out of the dominion of darkness. A new race of Spirit-born, Spirit-dominant, always restful, spiritually perceptive mankind has been exalted to sit beside Jesus who occupies the highest position, as we saw in Ephesians 2:6.

And God raised us up with Christ and seated us with him in the heavenly realms in Christ Jesus, in order that in the coming ages he might show the incomparable riches of his grace, expressed in his kindness to us in Christ Jesus.

That verse makes it clear we are not only His companions, not only His deputies to rule the earth as we were made to do, but also His showpiece for all the heavenly occupants to see. It's as if He points to us to notify them.

I imagine the humiliation to His enemies, as our Father holds us near and says, "Well, what you thought to take, I have given. The position you thought yourself qualified for, now belongs to the least qualified. The glory and power that you used to oppose me, I have given to the weakest creatures."

This is why both Hannah and Mary sang God's praise in the way they did in I Samuel 2:4-8 and in Luke 1:51-53. These humble ones recognized His plan to defeat the mighty and the proud through the weak and humble.

The bows of the warriors are broken,
   but those who stumbled are armed with strength.
Those who were full hire themselves out for food,
   but those who were hungry hunger no more.
She who was barren has borne seven children,
   but she who has had many sons pines away.

The LORD brings death and makes alive;
   he brings down to the grave and raises up.
The LORD sends poverty and wealth;
   he humbles and he exalts.
He raises the poor from the dust
   and lifts the needy from the ash heap;
he seats them with princes
   and has them inherit a throne of honor.

He has performed mighty deeds with his arm;
he has scattered those who are proud in their inmost
thoughts.
He has brought down rulers from their thrones
but has lifted up the humble.
He has filled the hungry with good things
but has sent the rich away empty.

This is God's way. It's one reason Jesus put so much emphasis on being last in order to be first, which we covered in depth previously.

Can you not imagine the fits of jealousy and envy, the fits of rage, that the devil and the unseen enemies must feel? God humiliating the former top angel by lifting you up to the place he once held. What an amazing plan by our Father. No wonder we praise Him so much.

That former top angel, Lucifer, forsook his place. We saw in Ezekiel 28 and Isaiah 14 his origins and fall. The devil once considered himself best fit to be the central focus of all existence, rather than God. In Isaiah 14:9-12 & 16-21, God reveals the devil is now reduced and marginalized, with not even a grave to call home.

The grave below is all astir
to meet you at your coming;
it rouses the spirits of the departed to greet you—
all those who were leaders in the world;
it makes them rise from their thrones—
all those who were kings over the nations.
They will all respond,
they will say to you,
"You also have become weak, as we are;
you have become like us."
All your pomp has been brought down to the grave,
along with the noise of your harps;
maggots are spread out beneath you
and worms cover you.

How you have fallen from heaven,
*   O morning star, son of the dawn!*

Those who see you stare at you,
*   they ponder your fate:*
"Is this the man who shook the earth
*   and made kingdoms tremble,*
the man who made the world a desert,
*   who overthrew its cities*
*   and would not let his captives go home?"*

All the kings of the nations lie in state,
*   each in his own tomb.*
But you are cast out of your tomb
*   like a rejected branch;*
you are covered with the slain,
*   with those pierced by the sword,*
*   those who descend to the stones of the pit.*
Like a corpse trampled underfoot,
*   you will not join them in burial,*
for you have destroyed your land
*   and killed your people.*
The offspring of the wicked
*   will never be mentioned again.*
Prepare a place to slaughter his sons
*   for the sins of their forefathers;*
they are not to rise to inherit the land
*   and cover the earth with their cities.*

In the heavenlies, the witnesses will say, "is this really him? He doesn't look nearly so powerful." And this marginalized angelic enemy is showered so much attention from Christians today? In doing so, they are giving him exactly what he wants—their fear and their ineffectiveness to rule over him. Naturally he and the demons love promoting such deception about who you are, Christian. It's in their best interests to keep our blindfolds on as long as they can.

Remember what happened to him in Eden? He—unlike the man and woman—was cursed.

> So the LORD God said to the serpent, "Because you have done this,
>
> "Cursed are you above all the livestock
>   and all the wild animals!
> You will crawl on your belly
>   and you will eat dust
>   all the days of your life.
> And I will put enmity
>   between you and the woman,
>   and between your offspring and hers;
> he will crush your head,
>   and you will strike his heel."

No wonder our leader, Jesus, is so unafraid of the devil, as He says in John 15:30 & 16:11,

> the prince of this world now stands condemned.....the prince of this world is coming. He has no hold on me.

Is it any surprise that we inherit the promised supremacy and fearsomeness to our enemies? Consider the fearsomeness attributed to God's obedient people, from Leviticus 26:6-8 and Deuteronomy 28:7.

> ...no one will make you afraid. I will remove savage beasts from the land, and the sword will not pass through your country. You will pursue your enemies, and they will fall by the sword before you. Five of you will chase a hundred, and a hundred of

you will chase ten thousand, and your enemies will fall by the sword before you.

The LORD will grant that the enemies who rise up against you will be defeated before you. They will come at you from one direction but flee from you in seven.

This is evident for Israel during David's reign, in I Chronicles 14:16. There David's obedience is described, with this result:

David's fame spread throughout every land, and the LORD made all the nations fear him.

This was not the first time. Look at Rahab's description of the fearsomeness of the Israelites in Joshua 2:9 & 11.

I know that the LORD has given this land to you and that a great fear of you has fallen on us, so that all who live in this country are melting in fear because of you. ...When we heard of it, our hearts melted and everyone's courage failed because of you, for the LORD your God is God in heaven above and on the earth below.

Does that not sound remarkably similar to the way demons responded to Jesus? And so also to you. Let's see: God lives in you. You are born of the Holy Spirit of God. You are one of His new creation. You are never stuck in restlessness, but continually at rest with Him. You are an Earth-ruler. When you stack up these identities that you and all followers of Jesus share, no wonder our enemies are powerless before us. No wonder they have to go when we say go and where we say go.

You and your old identity might be taking an out here. You might be thinking that the above promises are rewards for obedience, and not applicable to you. So let's do like Jesus and judge that for what it is: "little faith." Of course, the promised authority and supremacy over enemies is for the obedient only! And you follow that Obedient One. It's not your obedience that qualifies you—it's His.

Far from usurping His position as the One Obedient Inheritor of the promised supremacy, you gladly stand behind Him in your poverty of spirit and meekness, do you not? For if He was our enemies' tormentors, are not we also, who follow Him? He said so Himself in Luke 10:18-19 and Mark 16:17.

He replied, "I saw Satan fall like lightning from heaven. I have given you authority to trample on snakes and scorpions and to overcome all the power of the enemy; nothing will harm you."

And these signs will accompany those who believe: In my name they will drive out demons

This truth was presented to John in Revelation 19:11-16—Jesus the Faithful & True, and us His armies behind, following Him.

I saw heaven standing open and there before me was a white horse, whose rider is called Faithful and True. With justice he judges and makes war. His eyes are like blazing fire, and on his head are many crowns. He has a name written on him that no one knows but he himself. He is dressed in a robe dipped in blood, and his name is the Word of God. The armies of heaven were following him, riding on white horses and dressed in fine linen, white and clean. Out of his mouth comes a sharp sword with which to strike down the nations. "He will rule them with an iron scepter." He treads the winepress of the fury of the wrath of God Almighty. On his robe and on his thigh he has this name written:

King of kings and Lord of lords.

Alright then—no more cowering for you, mighty warrior, free of blindfold. You are a king under the King of all kings. You are a lord under the Lord of all lords. And you are unblindfolded.

ACTIVATION 11-6

Let's walk your new thinking through its paces. Check your answer on each one.

❑Yes ❑No Is Jesus fearsome to demons?

❑Yes ❑No Is His follower fearsome to demons?

❑Yes ❑No Is Jesus undefeatable by demons?

❑Yes ❑No Is His follower undefeatable by demons?

❑Yes ❑No Is Jesus a conqueror of God's enemies?

Now read this, from Romans 8:35-39 and answer, "am I a conqueror of God's enemies?"

Who shall separate us from the love of Christ? Shall trouble or hardship or persecution or famine or nakedness or danger or sword? As it is written:

"For your sake we face death all day long;
*   we are considered as sheep to be slaughtered."*

No, in all these things we are more than conquerors through him who loved us. For I am convinced that neither death nor life, neither angels nor demons, neither the present nor the future, nor any powers, neither height nor depth, nor anything else in all creation, will be able to separate us from the love of God that is in Christ Jesus our Lord.

❑Yes ❑No Am I, as Jesus' follower, a conqueror of
          God's enemies?

❑Yes ❑No Did Jesus replace Lucifer as the one to exercise
          God's rule from heaven?

Sorry—I couldn't resist a trick question there. The answer to that one is "not exactly." Jesus as the Son of Man was first to supplant the devil's dominion. But he was not the last and only. He promptly handed it to us His Church. Jesus alone did not replace Lucifer as the chief executor of God's will. WE DID, with JESUS. In this light, consider Paul's wording for it in Ephesians 1:9-10, 22-23.

And he made known to us the mystery of his will according to his good pleasure, which he purposed in Christ, to be put into effect when the times will have reached their fulfillment— to bring all things in heaven and on earth together under one head, even Christ.

God placed all things under his feet and appointed him to be head over everything for the church, which is his body, the fullness of him who fills everything in every way.

That's what God showed Daniel 450 years before Jesus was even born, in Daniel 7:13-14 & 27.

In my vision at night I looked, and there before me was one like a son of man, coming with the clouds of heaven. He approached the Ancient of Days and was led into his presence. He was given authority, glory and sovereign power; all peoples, nations and men of every language worshiped him. His dominion is an everlasting dominion that will not pass away, and his kingdom is one that will never be destroyed.

Then the sovereignty, power and greatness of the kingdoms under the whole heaven will be handed over to the saints, the people of the Most High. His kingdom will be an everlasting kingdom, and all rulers will worship and obey him.

Handed over to the saints—that's us. Jesus knew this to be the outcome of His suffering. He was the beginning of the end for the unseen enemies, and He knew it.

Let's sum up what we have seen in Scripture so the biblical understanding of spiritual warfare can characterize you and make you effective.

Lucifer was second only to God (Ezekiel 28:12-14). But his pride squeezed out all his meekness for being second to anybody. (Isaiah 14:13-14, Ezekiel 28:2) He fell, is confined to earth and angry (Revelation 12:12, Luke 10:18). He is doomed with little time remaining to roam. And when all is done, who will occupy the place in heaven that he once held? Jesus' Bride the Church. Jesus received this by His utter humility, His weakness and His submission to the devil's worst weapon, death (Hebrews 2:14, Philippians 2:5-11). And to worsen matters for the devil, the perfect Man Jesus takes back people the devil had despoiled, and takes them to His high place in the heavenly realms (Ephesians 4:8-10, Psalm 68:15-18). And from that high seat, you and I are God's continual taunt to those former angels who dared to oppose Him. (Ephesians 2:6-7)

That puts things in perspective.

ACTIVATION 11-7

At the outset of the chapter, you named a person whose problems were so inescapable, repetitive or severe that demons seem to be involved. Write out a declaration that you, right now, can make, out loud, to terminate that oppression in that person's life.

_____

_____

_____

_____

_____

ACTIVATION 11-8

I asked you when the presence of evil close to you was inescapably perceptible. Write out a declaration to make, out loud, to repudiate the high place which that event has occupied in your memories.

_____

_____

_____

_____

_____

ACTIVATION 11-9

Write out a command for where you want to send that memory. Since you have dislodged it from its negative influence on your mind, send it somewhere. I was taught to send it where Jesus sends it.

_____

_____

_____

_____

_____

ACTIVATION 11-10

Do you remember I asked you to name the person of whom you would immediately think to bring an insurmountable evil obstacle? Now say this out loud with that person's name in the blank: _God has determined and decreed that I too, like_ _____ _am superior over evil as a follower of His Son, Jesus._

These last activations are vocal. How do you rule? By your will and your words. So let's make your body the servant of God's domination of the unseen enemies. Extend His influence by extending yours. Is this not why we raise our voice—to communicate more broadly?

Raise your voice like the lion roaring over his territory. Shout like a warrior rushing down upon the heads of the doomed.

ACTIVATION 11-11

Read these loudly!

I AM FEARSOME TO DEMONS.

I AM THEIR UNDEFEATABLE OPPONENT.

I AM THEIR FEARSOME REPLACEMENT.

I ASSIST JESUS IN EXTENDING HIS AUTHORITY OVER THEM.

I WILL ASSIST HIM AS A MEMBER OF HIS ARMY IN THE LAST DAYS.

Father, I see!

Praise you God!

I love your marvelous light!

EPILOGUE:
YOU ARE YOUR FATHER'S CHILD

Everything you have read is dynamite. Its only proper use is to help you believe, receive and activate what God has revealed about you in the Bible: you are your Father's child. What He is, you are on this earth.

> *love is made complete among us so that we will have confidence on the day of judgment, because in this world we are like him.* (I John 4:17)

There are people who use these truths for their own purposes. Do not let yourself be one of them, for they are not meek, mourning, poor in spirit. The dynamite God put into these truths has a destructive effect on those who misuse it.

But in your hands, living as your Father's child, these truths are the dynamite that moves mountains. With your blindfold removed, you see that through Him, your identity removes obstacles, raises valleys, builds up the road, and prepares the way for the Lord. You gather, not scatter.

Everything you have read about yourself is only possible because Jesus' Father is your Father, and because Jesus is your first-born Brother (Hebrews 2:11). So imagine the moment, the feelings of Jesus when He first arose from the dead! The power! The vigor! The joy! The unassailable life He must have felt coursing through His veins!

So it's noteworthy, what He wanted to talk about. What was the first subject when He encountered people for the first time? Matthew 27:9-10 and John 20:17 record for us His first attention.

Suddenly Jesus met them. "Greetings," he said. They came to him, clasped his feet and worshiped him. Then Jesus said to them, "Do not be afraid. Go and tell my brothers to go to Galilee; there they will see me."

Jesus said, "Do not hold on to me, for I have not yet returned to the Father. Go instead to my brothers and tell them, 'I am returning to my Father and your Father, to my God and your God.'"

Do you know Jesus to be that excited about *you*? That kind of brother to you, that His first thought is for His brothers? That is who He is. That is who you are.

Your Father is the only determiner of who you are, Christian, because you are in His image, He lives in you, and Jesus is the first-born Brother of many such people. Be your Father's child. That's all.

You may have been trained to think of Him as "The Father." You might have located Him out there somewhere, or all around. Can you make the shift to live with Him as "my Father" who is in you right now and always? That's what Jesus' words tell you to do—*my Father and your Father*.

You may have been transactional. Maybe you saw Him in a tit-for-tat relationship with you. You may have thought He was running events like a puppeteer dangles the strings of a marionette, sizing up your every thought and action. Your training might have been to give Him what He wants so you can get what you want. Now however you see your biblical confidence relationship with Him. Now you can run to Him right in your own heart for He is there never to leave, no conditions but to see you in His Son, Jesus.

Books and conferences offer truths and training that are valuable, for sure. But the sign that you are maturing well is that you get eyes only for your Father. The attraction of the things you've read about in this book will become no more than simple, customary elements of your continual, confident relationship with your Father. They will be just a few more of the many ways He expresses, through you, His sovereignty over everything.

Your Father loves you. What more is there to say? So say this often and always:

I AM MY FATHER'S CHILD

Daddy God, I love you.
Son, I love you.

Whether you want to purchase bulk copies of
Christian, What Are You?
or buy another book for a friend, get it now at:
www.christianwhatareyou.com

If you have a book that you would like to publish,
contact Jon McHatton, Publisher, at A Book's Mind,
jon@abooksmind.com
www.abooksmind.com